THOMAS MERTON

M. Basil Pennington (ed.)

THOMAS MERTON

I Have Seen
What I Was Looking For

Selected Spiritual Writings

New City Press
Hyde Park, NY

Published in the United States by New City Press
202 Cardinal Rd., Hyde Park, NY 12538
www.newcitypress.com
©2005 Cistercian Abbey of Spencer, Inc.

Cover design by Durvanorte Correia
Cover photo of Thomas Merton: John Howard Griffin
    used by permission of the Merton Legacy Trust

Library of Congress Cataloging-in-Publication Data:

Merton, Thomas, 1915-1968.
  [Selections. 2005]
  Thomas Merton: I have seen what I was looking for : selected spiritual writings / M. Basil
Pennington, ed[itor].
    p. cm.
  ISBN 1-56548-225-5 (alk. paper)
  1. Spiritual life--Catholic Church. 2. Merton, Thomas, 1915-1968. I. Pennington, M. Basil.
II. Title.
  BX2182.3.M47   2005
  271'.12502--dc22

                                    2005004241

Printed in the United States of America

Contents

Welcome

A monk, a mystic — yes! A merry, mischievous monk and a modern, muddied mystic. Deadly intent upon becoming a saint — what else is there to do — knowing that a can of beer is a help along the way. Tom Merton, with all the class of a Cambridge dropout and all the earthiness of a World's Fair barker, didn't miss much of life and he never dropped out of life. However he did live through phases like any other man under the moon.

I am not going to take much space here telling the man's story; he tells it better himself, through his most revealing writings. A chronology can be found at the end of this book if you want to study the geography of his life.

The public school youth who wrote a paper on Gandhi in the 1930s showed exceptional precocity. This paper which unfortunately has not survived for our study probably is a truer and more authentic witness to young Thomas Merton's social concern and compassion than the fact that he displayed a copy of Karl Marx prominently on his desk. But whatever seeds of compassion the great Indian leader might have sown in Merton lay dormant under a heavy layer of hedonism for some years. The exciting marches that marked life in

Cambridge in the early 1930s did not benefit from Merton's participation. He was too busy partying or sleeping off the previous night's excesses.

Failure, disgrace, and exile brought a wiser Merton to Columbia University, New York in 1935. Here he did participate actively in some political and social demonstrations. For a brief period he even joined the Communist Party, leaving it more because of the other members' lack of seriousness than because of any lack on his part. With deadly earnestness (He struggled with the urge toward suicide on at least one occasion.) Merton set out on a quest for meaning as death after death marked his young life and he found himself more and more alone. He led his few friends, rather than being led by them, which is not to say he did not learn from them and grow through their friendship. He was blessed with some good mentors (Mark Van Doren, Dan Walsh and Abbot Frederic Dunne most significantly) who helped him to grow and to find some of the answers he sought. Though, as Merton himself said, minds from the past whom he contacted through his voluminous reading probably had the greater influence on him, an odd mix: Gilson, Huxley, Blake, Hopkins, Bernard of Clairvaux, Aquinas, Scotus, to name only a few. Prejudice gave way to faith. And the discipline of faith, with its grace and hope, gradually broke open the soil for the seeds of compassion to sprout.

When Catherine de Hueck came to the campus of Saint Bonaventure (where Merton was teaching) in the summer of 1941 Merton was ready to hear her. At her bidding he came to Friendship House in Harlem (an outreach to the poorest and most needy started by de Hueck) for a look-see and began to consider this seriously as a vocation. But something else was tugging at the young professor's heart. It was a lofty ideal that, not yet fully understood, was able to marshal the self-interest of the false self in its cause. The attractive image of the contemplative saint won out over that of the self-giving apostle. A false hierarchy of values still prevalent within the Catholic community undoubtedly influenced this decision. But for those who love God all things work together unto good. God would have his way with this young man who was being seduced into a way that would prove more demanding, purifying and effective, given the special talents the Master had bestowed upon his disciple.

Thomas Merton's closest friend, Bob Lax, knew him well and well expressed what was going on:

> When he [Merton] first got to the monastery he might have thought that he could live just a contemplative life cut off from the rest of the world. That may have been an illusion that . . . anyone could expect would soon wear off. . . . When he got back to a more universal point of view . . . that was the Merton we already knew before he got there and it was just part of him coming back.

During his earliest monastic days Merton did try to deny parts of himself and most of the world. He needed a breakthrough to get "back to a more universal point of view." In a way, another tradition opened the way for him: the rich Christian tradition of the Byzantine East. He had long been in touch with this tradition in various ways: the icons at Rome, his father's drawings, the Cistercian Fathers, his study of the Fathers of the Desert. In the early 1950s he had an opportunity to study the Eastern Christian Fathers more fully and reflect more profoundly on them as he prepared and gave a course to his fellow monks. We have his notes from this course. Here, he got his breakthrough insight into *theoria physike* under the tutelage of Evagrius Ponticus and Maximus the Confessor. His understanding of *theoria physike* — a spiritualized knowledge of the created, a sort of natural con-templation, which reaches to the divine *oikonomia*, God's plan for things, and the *logoi* of things, the divine place within things — enabled the zealous, ascetic, world-despising young monk to reintegrate his natural gifts and disposition towards compassion, his love for all that God made, so that he could go on to become the full and integrated person he became, a man of truest compassion. Merton's "discovery" and full percep-tion of *theoria physike* had a profound formative and liberating influence on him. This is evident in the book he produced shortly after this, *The New Man*. When Dan Walsh, who had known Merton for about twenty years, read the volume, he exclaimed, *"The New Man* — the new Merton."

But what was still perhaps too theoretical moved forward to becoming a powerful motivating force in Merton's life through a Jungian experience. Merton himself will tell you about it in his letter to Boris Pasternak. After this Merton no longer sought to be a heroic ascetic, a model monk, but rather a man of love, of compassion, of presence, even if the righ-teous were scandalized. Before the experience of March 18, 1958, Merton would write of "the indignity of being a member of the human race"; after, he would write, "It is a glorious destiny to be a member of the human race." Before he would write, "The contemplative and the Marxist have no common ground"; he devoted his last talk to monasticism and Marxism. He would now praise de Chardin for proclaiming the Good News in a way that both scientists and Marxists could accept. He would join Teilhard in his prayer "to be widely human in my sympathies and more nobly terrestrial with my ambitions than any of the world's servants." He had entered into his depths and found one Person drawing all together into a common humanity, all part of one creation, all coming forth from one heart, the heart of God-Christ.

As Merton stepped further apart from his monastic community and in that respect further from society, to find greater freedom, he found a greater freedom to be with others. In the first days of 1964 he wrote in his journal: "I need to find my way out of a constructed solitude which is actually the chief obstacle to realization of true solitude in openness and inner subjectivity. False solitude is built on an artificially induced awareness of unrealized possibilities of relationship with others. One prefers to keep these possibilities unrealized. (Hence, false solitude is a short-circuit to love.)."

Merton was not a southerner but he lived half his life in the south and the plight of the blacks was very present to him. When his consciousness expanded he entered fully into Martin Luther King's non-violent crusade. He put his pen at the service of the cause. Such poems as "And the Children of Birmingham" and "Picture of a Black Child with a White Doll" tear at the heart. "Letters to a White Liberal" and "The Legend of Tucker Caliban" amply express his hopes and his frustrations with the Black Revolution. He felt the Church, the Christian community as a whole and white liberals had failed the blacks and he understood their turning to the Black Muslims.

Merton's compassion reached out to all victims: the victims of the racism that surrounded him in the south of the United States, the victims of the Holocaust; the victims of the bomb; the victims of the Vietnam war. He entered deeply into the experience of individuals. His many writings offer the most ample witness to Merton's universal compassion. The expressions of it are profoundly beautiful at times. But he most powerfully gives witness to the ground and root of true compassion, namely a keen awareness of our common humanity, our oneness in God and God's loving design upon us, a design that calls for a unity that becomes a oneness in God.

As we page through the vast richness of Merton's literary
heritage we can hear something of the huge chorus of living
beings. Nature speaks through his early poetry with a gentleness and a charm that may have been somewhat lost in his
later, more powerful poetic prose and anti-poetry, but nature
continued to speak out, especially in the joys of his journaling.
The volumes of his letters let us hear echoes of the voices of
human persons, delightfully young and sapiently old, rich
and poor in this world's goods and in the riches of the spirit,
persons of high station and low, well known and hidden —
they are all there in an array that amazes. As we have indicated we especially hear through Merton the cries of the
oppressed: Jews, blacks, Native Americans, victims of war . . .
and so many others. He gives voice to activists, and to philosophers and poets without number. We hear the voice of the
Church; he translated papal encyclicals and ecclesial docu-
ments and shared the resonance they awakened within his
spirit. He gave voice to theologians: Catholic, Protestant,
Jewish and Muslim; and Hindu, Buddhist and Taoist, if we
can properly speak of theology in these traditions. The Fathers
of the Church and his own Cistercian Fathers, whom he loved
so well, were deeply heard and allowed to speak again
through him. Even more did he hear the divinely inspired
words of the Bible and share insights that smoothly but inci-
sively cut right through to the core of our being. Above all does
he give voice to the silence of contemplation, the contemplative experience of God, the Creator and conductor of the huge
chorus of living creatures, who deftly leads them into the
creation and exultation of a new world.

Thomas Merton listened with an exquisitely fine and developed listening and heard the voice of a new world, a voice that
spoke of promise and inspired hope. And he had a fine and
developed ability to give that voice a new voice in the written
word. That is why we want to listen to Thomas Merton. We

cannot give a complete Merton bibliography in this volume, for that takes a volume in itself; but the chronology will mention many of his books.

In an essay about Saint Aelred of Rievaulx, one of the early Cistercian writers, Merton describes what he sees to be the sources of the genius of the great Cistercian writers of the twelfth century. The passage can be applied in detail to Merton himself as one of the great Cistercian writers of the twentieth century:

> The rich and elegant vitality of Cistercian prose — most of which is sheer poetry — betrays an overflow of literary productivity which did not even need to strive for its effects: it achieved them, as it were, spontaneously. It seemed to be second nature to St. Bernard, William of St. Thierry, Adam of Perseigne, Guerric of Igny [and we would add, Louis of Gethsemani — better known as Thomas Merton] to write with consummate beauty prose full of sound and color and charm. There were two natural explanations for this. The first is that the prolific Cistercian writers of the Golden Age were men who had already been thoroughly steeped in the secular literary movements of the time before they entered the cloister. All of them had rich experience of the current of humanism that flowered through the twelfth-century renaissance. . . . There is a second explanation for the richness and exuberance of theological prose in twelfth-century monasteries of Citeaux. If contact with classical humanism had stimulated a certain intellectual vitality in these clerics, it also generated a conflict in their souls. The refined natural excitements produced by philosophical speculation, by art,

poetry, music, by the companionship of restless, sensitive and intellectual friends merely unsettled their souls. Far from finding peace and satisfaction in all these things, they found war. The only answer to the problem was to make a clean break with everything that stimulated this spiritual uneasiness, to withdraw from the centers in which it was fomented, and get away somewhere, discover some point of vantage from which they could see the whole difficulty in its proper perspective. This vantage point, of course, was not only the cloister, since Ovid and Tully had already become firmly established there, but the desert — the *terra invia et inaquosa* in which the Cistercian labored and suffered and prayed. . . . The tension generated by the conflict between secular humanism and the Cistercian humanism, which seeks the fulfillment of human nature through ascetic renunciation and mystical union with God, was one of the proximate causes of the powerful mystical writing of the Cistercians. However, once these two natural factors have been considered, we must recognize other and far more decisive influences, belonging to a higher order. . . . It is the relish and savor that only experience can give that communicates to the writings of the twelfth-century Cistercians all the vitality and vividness and impassioned sincerity which are peculiarly their own. . . . The White Monks speak with accents of a more personal and more lyrical conviction that everywhere betrays the influence of an intimate and mystical experience. . . . It is the personal experiential character of Cistercian mysticism that gives the prose of the White Monks its vivid freshness. . . . Since the theology of the Cistercians was so intimately personal and experiential, their exposition of it was bound to take a psychological direction. All that they wrote was directed by their keen awareness of the presence and action of God in their souls. This was their all absorbing interest.

It is sometimes surprising to students of Merton to discover that this man who published not only an autobiography but also a whole series of journals or quasi-journals was in fact a very private person. The autobiography and the journals were carefully edited works, the fruit of rather selective editing, to some extent an editing required by the censors of his order but far more extensively an editing required by his own innate need for privacy. Now that the journals that were sealed for twenty-five years after his death and his letters have been published we can get a far more candid picture of the man. His letters tended to go straight from his heart through the typewriter to the recipient. The deeper the spiritual affinity Merton sensed with his correspondent, and it seemed too, the farther away the correspondent was, the more open Merton tended to be. One of his most personal revelations about his own prayer life is found in a letter to Aziz Ch. Abdul, a Sufi who lived on the other side of the earth. In a correspondence that had to spend months passing through the underground, a letter to Boris Pasternak, we are let in on the Jungian experience that effectively transformed Merton into a wide-open listener who clearly perceived the unifying principle within all.

Through a lifetime evolution he opened out till he no longer set any limits and God and all that is of God could enter in and be experienced in its oneness in the Divine. The experiences that brought Thomas Merton to this were many. Many were unique and will remain unique to his truly unique life-journey. Yet essentially it was in his practice of contemplation that he continually let go and allowed the Divine the freedom to open him out ever more, enlightening him through the activity of the Spirit; it enabled him to come to see — or rather to hear the true synthesis of all in the harmony of the huge chorus of living beings and in the midst of it live out a vision of a new world where all division has fallen away and the divine goodness is perceived and enjoyed as present in all and through all.

For whom then is this quite limited anthology drawn from the writings of Thomas Merton intended?

Certainly it offers a good place for a beginner to get acquainted with Thomas Merton. Far better to get to know him first through his own words than through the interpretations of others. I unashamedly include those favored pieces that we never tire of reading. They will be as savory to the beginner as they are to us long-time friends of Merton. But there is none-theless an overall sampling of the monk's writings.

The collection has something to offer though to those who look to Merton as a spiritual master, or to use the more tradi-tional title, a Spiritual Father. (Merton enjoyed for many years the monastic title of Father Master, a combination of the two.) It gives a considerable amount of space to gathering together some of our Father Master's most pertinent wisdom on the art or more truly the life of prayer. These concise excerpts offer us the words we can profitably hear again and again to feed and encourage our life of prayer.

No matter who the reader is, it is hoped this sampling will prove an effective encouragement to move on to the Master. And it may help many decide where they want to enter into the enormous and enormously rich literary heritage that Merton has left to us.

M. Basil Pennington, o.c.s.o.

The Autobiography
— And On It Went

At first glance it would seem a biographer of Thomas Merton has an embarrassment of riches: an autobiography and journals that cover his daily life through most of the years following its publication. Yet how many years did we have to wait after the publication of the autobiography to find out that Merton had a son or to hear anything about his relationship with "the nurse." As significant as these human details of Merton's life might seem, in fact they are relatively passing events in the journey of this Spiritual Master. And how much of that deeper journey has been left untold, perhaps as much from the impossibility of communicating it as from the modesty or reticence of the prolific author? Nonetheless I think letting the author, especially when he is as capable an author as Thomas Merton, tell his own story, revealing to us what he chooses to reveal, has its merits.

In this first section select passages from his famous and most successful autobiography and from his published journals, complemented by a few significant passages from his letters quickly take us along his journey up to the time of his "enlightenment" on the corner of Fourth and Walnut (now Muhammad Ali — Merton would like that!) on March 18, 1958.

Free by Nature in the Image of God

On the last day of January 1915, under the sign of the Water Bearer, in a year of a great war, and down in the shadow of some French mountains on the borders of Spain, I came into the world. Free by nature, in the image of God, I was nevertheless the prisoner of my own violence and my own selfishness, in the image of the world into which I was born. That world was the picture of Hell, full of men like myself, loving God and yet hating him; born to love him, living instead in fear and hopeless self-contradictory hungers.

Not many hundreds of miles away from the house where I was born, they were picking up the men who rotted in the rainy ditches among the dead horses and the ruined seventy-fives, in the forest of trees without branches along the river Marne.

My father and mother were captives in that world, knowing they did not belong with it or in it, and yet unable to get away from it. They were in the world and not of it — not because they were saints, but in a different way: because they were artists. The integrity of an artist lifts a man above the level of the world without delivering him from it.

My father painted like Cezanne and understood the southern French landscape the way Cezanne did. His vision of the world was sane, full of balance, full of veneration for structure, for the relations of masses and for all the circumstances that impress an individual identity on each created thing. His vision was religious and clean, and therefore his paintings were without decoration or superfluous comment, since a religious man respects the power of God's creation to bear witness for itself. My father was a very good artist.

Neither of my parents suffered from the little spooky prejudices that devour the people who know nothing but automobiles and movies and what's in the ice-box and what's in the papers and which neighbors are getting a divorce.

I inherited from my father his way of looking at things and some of his integrity and from my mother some of her dissatisfaction with the mess the world is in, and some of her versatility. From both I got capacities for work and vision and enjoyment and expression that ought to have made me some kind of a King, if the standards the world lives by were the real ones. Not that we ever had any money: but any fool knows that you don't need money to get enjoyment out of life.

If what most people take for granted were really true — if all you needed to be happy was to grab everything and see everything and investigate every experience and then talk about it, I should have been a very happy person, a spiritual millionaire, from the cradle even until now.

If happiness were merely a matter of natural gifts, I would never have entered a Trappist monastery when I came to the age of a man.

(*The Seven Storey Mountain*, pp. 3–4)

The Sorry Business Was All Over

All summer we went regularly and faithfully to the hospital once or twice a week. There was nothing we could do but sit there, and look at Father and tell him things which he could not answer. But he understood what we said.

In fact, if he could not talk, there were other things he could still do. One day I found his bed covered with little sheets of blue note paper on which he had been drawing. And the drawings were real drawings. But they were unlike anything he had ever done before — pictures of little irate Byzantine-looking saints with beards and great halos.

Of us all, Father was the only one who really had any kind of a faith. And I do not doubt that he had very much of it, and that behind the walls of his isolation, his intelligence and his will, unimpaired, and not hampered in any essential way by the partial obstruction of some of his senses, were turned to God, and communed with God who was with him and in him, and who gave him, as I believe, light to understand and to make use of his sufferings for his own good, and to perfect his soul. It was a great soul, large, full of natural charity. He was a man of exceptional intellectual honesty and sincerity and purity of understanding. And this affliction, this terrible and frightening illness which was relentlessly pressing him down even into the jaws of the tomb, was not destroying him after all.

Souls are like athletes, that need opponents worthy of them, if they are to be tried and extended and pushed to the full use of their powers, and rewarded according to their capacity. And my father was in a fight with this tumor, and none of us understood the battle. We thought he was done for, but it was making him great. And I think God was already weighing out to him the weight of reality that was to be his reward, for he certainly believed far more than any theologian would require of a man to hold explicitly as "necessity of means," and so he was eligible for this reward, and his struggle was authentic, and not wasted or lost or thrown away.

In the Christmas holidays I only saw him once or twice. Things were the same. I spent most of the holidays in Strasbourg, where Tom had arranged for me to go for the sake of the languages: German and French. I stayed in a big Protestant *pension* in the Rue Finkmatt, and was under the unofficial tutelage of a professor at the University, a friend of Tom's family and of the Protestant patriarch.

Professor Hering was a kind and pleasant man with a red beard, and one of the few Protestants I have met who struck

one as being at all holy: that is, he possessed a certain
profound interior peace, which he probably got from his
contact with the Fathers of the Church, for he was a teacher of
theology. We did not talk much about religion, however. Once
when some students were visiting him, one of them explained
to me the essentials of Unitarianism, and when I asked the
professor about it afterwards, he said it was all right, in a way
which indicated that he approved, in a sort of academic and
eclectic way, of all these different forms of belief; or rather
that he was interested in as objectively intriguing manifestations of a fundamental human instinct, regarding them more
or less through the eyes of a sociologist. As a matter of fact,
sometimes Protestant theology does in certain circumstances,
amount to little more than a combination of sociology and
religious history, but I will not accuse him of teaching it altogether in that sense, for I really have no idea how he taught it.

Under the inspiration of the environment, I went to the
Lutheran church and sat through a long sermon in German
which I did not understand. But I think that was all the
worship of God I did in Strasbourg. I was more interested in
Josephine Baker, a big skinny colored girl from some American city like St. Louis, who came to one of theaters and sang
J'ai deux amours, mon pays et Paris.

So I went back to school, after seeing Father for a moment
on the way through London. I had been back for barely a week
when I was summoned, one morning, to the Headmaster's
study, and he gave me a telegram which said that Father was
dead.

The sorry business was all over. And my mind made
nothing of it. There was nothing I seemed to be able to grasp.
Here was a man with a wonderful mind and a great talent and
a great heart: and, what was more, he was a man who had
brought me into the world, and had nourished me and cared
for me and had shaped my soul and to whom I was bound by

every possible kind of bond of affection and attachment and admiration and reverence: killed by a growth on his brain.

(*The Seven Storey Mountain*, pp. 83–84)

I Had a Long Way to Go

I had a long way to go. I had more to cross than the Atlantic. Perhaps the Styx, being only a river, does not seem so terribly wide. It is not its width that makes it difficult to cross, especially when you are trying to get out of hell, and not in. And so, this time, even though I got out of Europe, I still remained in hell. But it was not for want of trying.

It was a stormy crossing. When it was possible, I walked on the wide, empty decks that streamed with spray. Or I would get up forward where I could see the bows blast their way headfirst into the mountains of water that bore down upon us. And I would hang on to the rail while the ship reeled and soared into the wet sky, riding the sea that swept under us while every stanchion and bulkhead groaned and complained.

When we got on to the Grand Banks, the sea calmed and there was a fall of snow, and the snow lay on the quiet decks, and made them white in the darkness of the evening. And because of the peacefulness of the snow, I imagined that my new ideas were breeding within me an interior grace.

The truth is, I was in the thick of a conversion. It was not the right conversion, but it was a conversion. Perhaps it was a lesser evil. I do not doubt much that it was. But it was not, for all that, much of a good. I was becoming a Communist.

Stated like that, it sounds pretty much the same as if I said: "I was growing a moustache." As a matter of fact, I was still unable to grow a moustache. Or I did not dare try. And, I suppose, my Communism was about as mature as my face —

as the sour, perplexed, English face in the photo on my quota card. However, as far as I know, this was about as sincere and complete a step to moral conversion as I was then able to make with my own lights and desires, such as they then were.

A lot of things had happened to me since I had left the relative seclusion of Oakham, and had been free to indulge all my appetites in the world, and the time had come for a big readjustment in my values. I could not evade that truth. I was too miserable, and it was evident that there was too much wrong with my strange, vague, selfish hedonism.

It did not take very much reflection on the year I had spent at Cambridge to show me that all my dreams of fantastic pleasures and delights were crazy and absurd, and that everything I had reached out for had turned to ashes in my hands, and that I myself, into the bargain, had turned out to be an extremely unpleasant sort of person — vain, self-centered, dissolute, weak, irresolute, undisciplined, sensual, obscene and proud. I was a mess. Even the sight of my own face in a mirror was enough to disgust me.

When I came to ask myself the reasons for all this, the ground was well prepared. My mind was already facing what seemed to be an open door out of my spiritual jail. It was some four years since I had first read the Communist Manifesto, and I had never entirely forgotten about it. One of those Christmas vacations at Strasbourg I read some books about Soviet Russia, how all the factories were working overtime, and all the ex-moujiks wore great big smiles on their faces, welcoming Russian aviators on their return from Polar flights, bearing the boughs of trees in their hands. Then I often went to Russian movies, which were pretty good from the technical point of view, although probably not so good as I thought they were, in my great anxiety to approve of them.

Finally, I had in my mind the myth that Soviet Russia was the friend of all the arts, and the only place where true art could find a refuge in a world of bourgeois ugliness. Where I ever got that idea is hard to find out, and how I managed to cling to it for so long is harder still, when you consider all the photographs there were, for everyone to see, showing the Red Square with gigantic pictures of Stalin hanging on the walls of the world's ugliest buildings — not to mention the views of the projected monster monument to Lenin, like a huge mountain of soap-sculpture, and the Little Father of Communism standing on top of it, and sticking out one of his hands. Then, when I went to New York in the summer, I found the *New Masses* lying around the studios of my friends and, as a matter of fact, a lot of people I met were either party members or close to being so.

So now, when the time came for me to take spiritual stock of myself, it was natural that I should do so by projecting my whole spiritual condition into the sphere of economic history and the class-struggle. In other words, the conclusion I came to was that it was not so much I myself that was to blame for my unhappiness but the society in which I lived.

I considered the person that I now was, the person that I had been at Cambridge, and that I had made of myself, and I saw clearly enough that I was the product of my times, my society and my class.

(*The Seven Storey Mountain*, pp. 131–133)

What Are You Waiting For?

The days went on and the radios returned to their separate and individual murmuring, not to be regimented back into their appalling shout for yet another year. September, as I think, must have been more than half gone.

I borrowed Father Leahy's life of Hopkins from the library. It was a rainy day. I had been working in the library in the morning. I had gone to buy a thirty-five-cent lunch at one of those little pious kitchens on Broadway — the one where Professor Gerig, of the graduate school of French, sat daily in silence with his ancient, ailing mother, over a very small table, eating his Brussels sprouts. Later in the afternoon, perhaps about four, I would have to go down to Central Park West and give a Latin lesson to a youth who was sick in bed, and who ordinarily came to the tutoring school run by my landlord, on the ground floor of the house where I lived.

I walked back to my room. The rain was falling gently on the empty tennis courts across the street, and the huge old domed library stood entrenched in its own dreary greyness, arching a cyclops eyebrow at South Field. I took up the book about Gerard Manley Hopkins. The chapter told of Hopkins at Balliol, at Oxford. He was thinking of becoming a Catholic. He was writing letters to Cardinal Newman (not yet a cardinal) about becoming a Catholic.

All of a sudden, something began to stir within me, something began to push me, to prompt me. It was a movement that spoke like a voice.

"What are you waiting for?" it said. "Why are you sitting here? Why do you still hesitate? You know what you ought to do? Why don't you do it?"

I stirred in the chair, I lit a cigarette, looked out the window at the rain, tried to shut the voice up. "Don't act on impulses," I thought. "This is crazy. This is not rational. Read your book."

Hopkins was writing to Newman, at Birmingham, about his indecision.

"What are you waiting for?" said the voice within me again. "Why are you sitting there? It is useless to hesitate any longer. Why don't you get up and go?"

I got up and walked restlessly around the room. "It's absurd," I thought. "Anyway, Father Ford would not be there at this time of day. I would only be wasting time."

Hopkins had written to Newman, and Newman had replied to him, telling him to come and see him in Birmingham.

Suddenly, I could bear it no longer. I put down the book, and got into my raincoat, and started down the stairs. I went out into the street. I crossed over, and walked along by the grey wooden fence, towards Broadway, in the light rain.

And then everything inside me began to sing — to sing with peace, to sing with strength and to sing with conviction.

I had nine blocks to walk. Then I turned the corner of 121st Street, and the brick church and presbytery were before me. I stood in the doorway and rang the bell and waited.

When the maid opened the door, I said:

"May I see Father Ford, please?"

"But Father Ford is out."

I thought: well, it is not a waste of time, anyway. And I asked when she expected him back. I would come back later, I thought.

The maid closed the door. I stepped back into the street. And then I saw Father Ford coming around the corner from Broadway. He approached, with his head down, in a rapid thoughtful walk. I went to meet him and said:

"Father, may I speak to you about something?"

"Yes," he said, looking up, surprised. "Yes, sure, come into the house."

We sat in the little parlor by the door. And I said: "Father, I want to become a Catholic." . . .

As November began, my mind was taken up with this one thought: of getting baptized and entering at last into the supernatural life of the Church. In spite of all my studying and all my reading and all my talking, I was still infinitely poor and wretched in my appreciation of what was about to take place within me. I was about to set foot on the shore at the foot of the high, seven-circled mountain of a Purgatory steeper and more arduous than I was able to imagine, and I was not at all aware of the climbing I was about to have to do.

The essential thing was to begin the climb. Baptism was that beginning, and a most generous one, on the part of God. For, although I was baptized conditionally, I hope that his mercy swallowed up all the guilt and temporal punishment of my twenty-three black years of sin in the waters of the font, and allowed me a new start. But my human nature, my weakness, and the cast of my evil habits still remained to be fought and overcome.

Towards the end of the first week in November, Father Moore told me I would be baptized on the sixteenth. I walked out of the rectory that evening happier and more contented than I had ever been in my life. I looked at a calendar to see what saint had that day for a feast, and it was marked for St. Gertrude.

It was only in the last days before being liberated from my slavery to death, that I had the grace to feel something of my own weakness and helplessness. It was not a very vivid light that was given to me on the subject: but I was really aware, at last, of what a poor and miserable thing I was. On the night of the fifteenth of November, the eve of my Baptism and First Communion, I lay in my bed awake and timorous for fear that something might go wrong the next day. And to humiliate me still further, as I lay there, fear came over me that I might not be able to keep the eucharistic fast. It meant only going from midnight to ten o'clock without drinking any water or taking any food, yet all of a sudden this little act of self-denial which amounts to no more, in reality, than a sort of an abstract token, a gesture of goodwill, grew in my imagination until it seemed to be utterly beyond my strength — as if I were about to go without food and drink for ten days, instead of ten hours. I had enough sense left to realize that this was one of those curious psychological reactions with which our nature, not without help from the devil, tries to confuse us and avoid what reason and our will demand of it, and so I forgot about it all and went to sleep.

In the morning, when I got up, having forgotten to ask Father Moore if washing your teeth was against the eucharistic fast or not, I did not wash them, and, facing a similar problem about cigarettes, I resisted the temptation to smoke.

I went downstairs and out into the street to go to my happy execution and rebirth.

The sky was bright and cold. The river glittered like steel. There was a clean wind in the street. It was one of those fall days full of life and triumph, made for great beginnings, and yet I was not altogether excited: for there were still in my mind these vague, half animal apprehensions about the externals of what was to happen in the church — would my mouth be so dry that I could not swallow the Host? If that happened, what would I do? I did not know.

Gerdy joined me as I was turning in to Broadway. I do not remember whether Ed Rice caught up with us on Broadway of not. Lax and Seymour came after we were in church.

Ed Rice was my godfather. He was the only Catholic among us — the only Catholic among all my close friends. Lax, Seymour, and Gerdy were Jews. They were very quiet, and so was I. Rice was the only one who was not cowed or embarrassed or shy.

The whole thing was very simple. First of all, I knelt at the altar of Our Lady where Father Moore received my abjuration of heresy and schism. Then we went to the baptistery, in a little dark corner by the main door.

I stood at the threshold.

"What do you seek from the Church of God?" asked Father Moore.

"Faith!"

"What will faith bring you?"

"Life eternal."

Then the young priest began to pray in Latin, looking earnestly and calmly at the page of the *Rituale* through the lenses of his glasses. And I, who was asking eternal life, stood and watched him, catching a word of the Latin here and there.

He turned to me:

"Do you renounce Satan?"

In a triple vow I renounced Satan and his pomps and his works.

"Dost thou believe in God the Father almighty, Creator of heaven and earth?"

"Credo!" [I believe!]

Dost thou believe in Jesus Christ his only Son, who was born and suffered?"

"*Credo!*"

"Dost thou believe in the Holy Spirit, in the holy Catholic Church, the Communion of Saints, the remission of sins, the resurrection of the body and eternal life?"

"*Credo!*"

What mountains were falling from my shoulders! What scales of dark night were peeling off my intellect, to let in the inward vision of God and his truth! But I was absorbed in the liturgy, and waiting for the next ceremony. It had been one of the things that had rather frightened me — or rather, which frightened the legion that had been living in me for twenty-three years.

Now the priest blew into my face. He said: "*Exi ab eo, spiritus immunde*: Depart from him, thou impure spirit, and give place to the Holy Spirit, the Paraclete."

It was the exorcism. I did not see them leaving, but there must have been more than seven of them. I had never been able to count them. Would they ever come back? Would that terrible threat of Christ be fulfilled, that threat about the man whose house was clean and garnished, only to be reoccupied by the first devil and many others worse than himself?

The priest, and Christ in him — for it was Christ that was doing these things through his visible ministry, in the Sacrament of my purification — breathed again into my face.

"Thomas, receive the good Spirit through this breathing, and receive the Blessing of God. Peace be with thee."

Then he began again to pray, and sign me with crosses, and presently came the salt which he put on my tongue — the salt of wisdom, that I might have the savor of divine things, and finally he poured the water on my head, and named me Thomas, "if thou be not already baptized."

After that, I went into the confessional, where one of the other assistants was waiting for me. I knelt in the shadows. Through the dark, close-meshed wire of the grille between us, I saw Father McGough, his head bowed, and resting on his hand, inclining his ear towards me. "Poor man," I thought. He seemed very young and he had always looked so innocent to me that I wondered how he was going to identify and understand the things I was about to tell him.

But one by one, that is, species by species, as best I could, I tore out all those sins by their roots, like teeth. Some of them were hard, but I did it quickly, doing the best I could to approximate the number of times all these things had happened — there was no counting them, only guessing.

I did not have any time to feel how relieved I was when I came stumbling out, as I had to go down to the front of the church where Father Moore would see me and come out to begin his — and my — Mass. But ever since that day, I have loved confessionals.

Now he was at the altar, in his white vestments, opening the book. I was kneeling right at the altar rail. The bright sanctuary was all mine. I could hear the murmur of the priest's voice, and the responses of the server, and it did not matter

that I had no one to look at, so that I could tell when to stand
and kneel down again, for I was still not very sure of these
ordinary ceremonies. But when the little bells were rung I
knew what was happening. And I saw the raised Host —
the silence and simplicity with which Christ once again
triumphed, raised up, drawing all things to himself —
drawing me to himself.

Presently the priest's voice was louder, saying the *Pater
Noster*. [Our Father] Then, soon, the server was running
through the *Confiteor* in a rapid murmur. That was for me,
Father Moore turned around and made a big cross in absolu-
tion, and held up the little Host.

"Behold the Lamb of God: behold him who taketh away the
sins of the world."

And my First Communion began to come towards me,
down the steps. I was the only one at the altar rail. Heaven was
entirely mine — that Heaven in which sharing makes no division or diminution. But this solitariness was a kind of re-
minder of the singleness with which this Christ, hidden in the
small Host, was giving himself for me, and to me, and, with
himself, the entire Godhead and Trinity — a great new in-
crease of the power and grasp of their indwelling that had
begun only a few minutes before at the font.

I left the altar rail and went back to the pew where the
others were kneeling like four shadows, four unrealities, and I
hid my face in my hands.

In the temple of God that I had just become, the One
Eternal and Pure Sacrifice was offered up to the God dwelling
in me: the sacrifice of God to God, and me sacrificed together
with God, incorporated in his Incarnation. Christ born in me,
a new Bethlehem, and sacrificed in me, his new Calvary, and
risen in me: offering me to the Father, in himself, asking the
Father, my Father and his, to receive me into his infinite and
special love — not the love he has for all things that exist — for

mere existence is a token of God's love, but the love of those creatures who are drawn to him in and with the power of his own love for himself.

For now I had entered into the everlasting movement of that gravitation which is the very life and spirit of God: God's own gravitation towards the depths of his own infinite nature, his goodness without end. And God, that center who is everywhere, and whose circumference is nowhere, finding me, through incorporation with Christ, incorporated into this immense and tremendous gravitational movement which is love, which is the Holy Spirit, loved me.

And he called out to me from his own immense depths.

(*The Seven Storey Mountain*, pp. 215–225)

La Caridad del Cobre Had a Word to Say to Me

In Santiago I ate dinner on the terrace of a big hotel in front of the cathedral. Across the square was the shell of a five-storey building that looked as if it had been gutted by a bomb: but the ruin had happened in an earthquake not so very long before. It was long enough ago so that the posters on the fence that had been put up in front of it had time to get tattered, and I was thinking: perhaps it is now getting to be time for another earthquake. And I looked up at the two towers of the cathedral, ready to sway and come booming down on my head.

The bus that took me to Cobre the next morning was the most dangerous of all the furious busses that are the terror of Cuba. I think it made most of the journey at eighty miles an hour on two wheels, and several times I thought it was going to explode. I said rosaries all the way up to the shrine, while the trees went by in a big greenish-yellow blur. If Our Lady had tried to appear to me, I probably would never even have gotten a glimpse of her.

I walked up the path that wound around the mound on which the Basilica stands. Entering the door, I was surprised that the floor was so shiny and the place so clean. I was in the back of the church, up in the apse, in a kind of oratory behind the high altar, and there, facing me, in a little shrine, was La Caridad, the little cheerful, black Virgin, crowned with a crown and dressed in royal robes, who is the Queen of Cuba.

There was nobody else in the place but a pious middle-aged lady attendant in a black dress who was eager to sell me a lot of medals and so I knelt before La Caridad and made my prayer and made my promise. I sneaked down into the Basilica after that, and knelt where I could see La Caridad and where I could really be alone and pray, but the pious lady, impatient to make her deal, or perhaps afraid that I might get up to some mischief in the Basilica, came down and peeked through the door.

So, disappointed and resigned, I got up and came out and bought a medal and got some change for the beggars and went away, without having a chance to say all that I wanted to say to La Caridad or to hear much from her.

Down in the village I bought a bottle of some kind of *gaseosa* and stood under the tin roof of the porch of the village store. Somewhere in one of the shacks, on a harmonium, was played: "*Kyrie Eleison, Kyrie Eleison, Kyrie Eleison.*"

And I went back to Santiago.

But while I was sitting on the terrace of the hotel, eating lunch, La Caridad del Cobre had a word to say to me. She handed me an idea for a poem that formed so easily and smoothly and spontaneously in my mind that all I had to do was finish eating and go up to my room and type it out, almost without a correction.

So the poem turned out to be both what she had to say to me and what I had to say to her. It was a song for La Caridad del Cobre, and it was, as far as I was concerned, something new, and the first real poem I had ever written, or anyway the one I like the best. It pointed the way to many other poems; it opened the gate, and set me traveling on a certain and direct track that was to last me several years.

The poem said:

> The white girls lift their heads like trees,
> The black girls go
> Reflected like flamingoes in the street.
> The white girls sing as shrill as water,
> The black girls talk as quiet as clay.
>
> The white girls open their arms like clouds,
> The black girls close their eyes like wings:
> Angels bow down like bells,
> Angels look up like toys,
> Because the heavenly stars
> Stand in a ring:
> And all the pieces of the mosaic, earth,
> Get up and fly away like birds.

When I went back to Havana, I found out something else, too, and something vastly more important. It was something that made me realize, all of a sudden, not merely intellectually, but experientially, the real uselessness of what I had been half deliberately looking for: the visions in the ceiba trees. And this experience opened another door, not a way to a kind of writing, but a way into a world infinitely new, a world that was out of this world of ours entirely and which transcended it infinitely, and which was not a world, but which was God himself.

I was in the Church of St. Francis in Havana. It was Sunday. I had been to Communion at some other church, I think at El

Cristo, and now I had come here to hear another Mass. The building was crowded. Up in the front, before the altar, there were rows and rows of children, crowded together. I forget whether they were First Communicants or not: but they were children around that age. I was far in the back of the church, but I could see the heads of all those children.

It came time for the Consecration. The priest raised the Host, then he raised the chalice. When he put the chalice down on the altar, suddenly a Friar in his brown robe and white cord stood up in front of the children, and all at once the voices of the children burst out:

"*Creo en Dios* . . ."

"I believe in God the Father Almighty, the creator of heaven and earth . . ."

The Creed. But that cry, "*Creo en Dios!*" It was loud, and bright and sudden and glad and triumphant; it was a good big shout, that came from all those Cuban children, a joyous affirmation of faith.

Then, as sudden as the shout and as definite, and a thousand times more bright, there formed in my mind an awareness, an understanding, a realization of what had just taken place on the altar, at the Consecration: a realization of God made present by the words of Consecration in a way that made him belong to me.

But what a thing it was, this awareness: it was so intangible, and yet it struck me like a thunderclap. It was a light that was so bright that it had no relation to any visible light and so profound and so intimate that it seemed like a neutralization of every lesser experience. And yet the thing that struck me most of all was that this light was in a certain sense "ordinary" — it was a light (and this most of all was what took my breath away) that was offered to all, to everybody, and there was nothing fancy or strange about it. It was the light of faith deepened and reduced to an extreme and sudden obviousness.

It was as if I had been suddenly illuminated by being blinded by the manifestation of God's presence.

The reason why this light was blinding and neutralizing was that there was and could be simply nothing in it of sense or imagination. When I call it a light that is a metaphor which I am using, long after the fact. But at the moment, another overwhelming thing about this awareness was that it disarmed all images, all metaphors, and cut through the whole skein of species and phantasms with which we naturally do our thinking. It ignored all sense experience in order to strike directly at the heart of truth, as if a sudden and immediate contact had been established between my intellect and the Truth who was now physically really and substantially before me on the altar. But this contact was not something speculative and abstract: it was concrete and experiential and belonged to the order of knowledge, yes, but more still to the order of love.

Another thing about it was that this light was something far above and beyond the level of any desire or any appetite I had ever yet been aware of. It was purified of all emotion and cleansed of everything that savored of sensible yearnings. It was love as clean and direct as vision: and it flew straight to the possession of the Truth I loved.

And the first articulate thought that came to my mind was: "Heaven is right here in front of me: Heaven, Heaven!"

(*The Seven Storey Mountain*, pp. 282–285)

The Time has Come for Me to Go and Be a Trappist

Three days went by with out any kind of an event. It was the end of November. All the days were short and dark.

Finally, on Thursday of that week, in the evening, I suddenly found myself filled with a vivid conviction:

"The time has come for me to go and be a Trappist."

Where had the thought come from? All I knew was that it was suddenly there. And it was something powerful, irresistible, clear.

I picked up a little book called *The Cistercian Life*, which I had bought at Gethsemani, and turned over the pages, as if they had something more to tell me. They seemed to me to be all written in words of flame and fire.

I went to supper, and came back and looked at the book again. My mind was literally full of this conviction. And yet, in the way, stood hesitation: that old business. But now there could be no delaying. I must finish with that, once and for all, and get an answer. I must talk to somebody who would settle it. It could be done in five minutes. And now was the time. Now.

Whom should I ask? Father Philotheus was probably in his room downstairs. I went downstairs, and out into the court. Yes, there was a light in Father Philotheus' room. All right. Go in and see what he has to say.

But instead of that, I bolted out into the darkness and made for the grove.

It was a Thursday night. The Alumni Hall was beginning to fill. They were going to have a movie. But I hardly noticed it: it did not occur to me that perhaps Father Philotheus might go to the movie with the rest. In the silence of the grove my feet were loud on the gravel. I walked and prayed. It was very, very dark by the shrine of the Little Flower. "For Heaven's sake, help me!" I said.

I started back towards the buildings. "All right. Now I am really going to go in there and ask him. Here's the situation, Father. What do you think? Should I go and be a Trappist?"

There was still a light in Father Philotheus' room. I walked bravely into the hall, but when I got within about six feet of his door it was almost as if someone had stopped me and held me where I was with physical hands. Something jammed in my will. I couldn't walk a step further, even though I wanted to. I made a kind of a push at the obstacle, which was perhaps a devil, and then turned around and ran out of the place once more.

And again I headed for the grove. The Alumni Hall was nearly full. My feet were loud on the gravel. I was in the silence of the grove, among wet trees.

I don't think there was ever a moment in my life when my soul felt so urgent and so special an anguish. I had been praying all the time, so I cannot say that I began to pray when I arrived there where the shrine was: but things became more definite.

"Please help me. What am I going to do? I can't go on like this. You can see that! Look at the state I am in. What ought I to do? Show me the way." As if I needed more information or some kind of a sign!

But I said this time to the Little Flower: "You show me what to do." And I added, "If I get into the monastery, I will be your monk. Now show me what to do."

It was getting to be precariously near the wrong way to pray — making indefinite promises that I did not quite understand and asking for some sort of a sign.

Suddenly, as soon as I had made that prayer, I became aware of the woods, the trees, the dark hills, the wet night wind, and then, clearer than any of these obvious realities, in my imagination, I started to hear the great bell of Gethsemani ringing in the night — the bell in the big grey tower, ringing and ringing, as if it were just behind the first hill. The impression made me breathless, and I had to think twice to realize that it was only in my imagination. that I was hearing the bell of the Trappist Abbey singing in the dark. Yet, as I afterwards calculated, it was just about that time that the bell is rung every night for the *Salve Regina*, toward the end of Compline.

The bell seemed to be telling me where I belonged — as if it were calling me home.

This fancy put such a determination into me as I immediately started back for the monastery — going the long way 'round, past the shrine of Our Lady of Lourdes and the far end of the football field. And with every step I took my mind became more and more firmly made up that now I would be done with all these doubts and hesitations and questions and all the rest, and get this thing settled, and go to the Trappists where I belonged.

When I came into the courtyard, I saw that the light in Father Philotheus' room was out. In fact, practically all the lights were out. Everybody had gone to the movies. My heart sank.

Yet there was one hope. I went right on through the door and into the corridor, and turned to the Friar's common room. I had never even gone near that door before. I had never dared. But now I went up and knocked on the glass panel and opened the door and looked inside.

There was nobody there except one Friar alone, Father Philotheus. I asked if I could speak with him and we went out to his room.

That was the end of all my anxiety, all my hesitation.

As soon as I proposed all my hesitations and questions to him, Father Philotheus said that he could see no reason why I shouldn't want to enter a monastery and become a priest.

It may seem irrational, but at the moment, it was as if scales fell off my own eyes, and looking back on all my worries and questions, I could see clearly how empty and futile they had been. Yes, it was obvious that I was called to the monastic life: and all my doubts about it had been mostly shadows. Where had they gained such a deceptive appearance of substance and reality? Accident and circumstances had all contributed to exaggerate and distort things in my mind. But now everything was straight again. And already I was full of peace and assurance — the consciousness that everything was right, and that a straight road had opened out, clear and smooth ahead of me.

Father Philotheus had only one question:

"Are you sure you want to be a *Trappist?*" he asked me.

"Father," I answered, "I want to give God everything."

I could see by the expression on his face that he was satisfied.

I went upstairs like somebody who had been called back from the dead. Never had I experienced the calm, untroubled peace and certainty that now filled my heart. There was only one more question: would the Trappists agree with Father Philotheus, and accept my application?

(*The Seven Storey Mountain*, pp. 363–366)

I Was Enclosed in . . . New Freedom

So Brother Matthew locked the gate behind me and I was enclosed in the four walls of my new freedom.

And it was appropriate that the beginning of freedom should be as it was. For I entered a garden that was dead and stripped and bare. The flowers that had been there last April were all gone. The sun was hidden behind low clouds and an icy wind was blowing over the grey grass and the concrete walks.

In a sense my freedom had already begun, for I minded none of these things. I did not come to Gethsemani for the flowers, or for the climate — although, I admit that the Kentucky winters were a disappointment. Still, I had not had time to plan on any kind of a climate. I had been too busy with the crucially important problem of finding out God's will. And that problem was still not entirely settled.

There still remained the final answer: would I be accepted into this monastery? Would they take me in to the novitiate, to become a Cistercian?

Father Joachim, the guest master, came out the door of the monastery and crossed the garden with his hands under his scapular and his eyes fixed on the cement walk. He only raised them when he was near me and then he grinned.

"Oh, it's you," he said. I suppose he had been doing some praying for me too.

I did not give him a chance to ask if I had come to stay. I said: "Yes, Father, this time I want to be a novice — if I can."

He just smiled. We went into the house. The place seemed very empty. I put the suitcase down in the room that had been assigned to me, and hastened to the church.

If I expected any grand welcome from Christ and his angels, I did not get it — not in the sensible order. The huge nave was like a tomb, and the building was as cold as ice. However, I did not mind. Nor was I upset by the fact that nothing special came into my head in the way of a prayer. I just knelt there more or less dumb, and listened to the saw down at the sawmill fill the air with long and strident complaints and the sound of labor.

That evening at supper I found that there was another postulant — an ancient, toothless, grey-haired man hunched up in a huge sweater. He was a farmer from the neighborhood who had lived in the shadow of the abbey for years and had finally made up his mind to enter it as a lay brother. However, he did not stay.

The next day I found out there was still a third postulant. He arrived that morning. He was a fat bewildered youth from Buffalo. Like myself, he was applying for the choir. Father Joachim put the two of us to work together washing dishes and waxing floors, in silence. We were both absorbed in our own many thoughts, and I dare say he was no more tempted to start a conversation than I was.

In fact every minute of the day I was secretly congratulating myself that conversations were over and done with — provided always I was accepted.

I could not be quite sure whether someone would call me and tell me to go down for an interview with the Father Abbot, or whether I was expected to go down to him on my own initiative, but that part of the problem was settled for me towards the end of the morning work.

I went back to my room and started puzzling my head over the copy of the *Spiritual Directory* that Father Joachim had brought me. Instead of settling down quietly and reading the chapter that directly concerned me, the one that said what postulants were supposed to do while they were waiting in the Guest House, I started leafing through the two thin volumes to see if I could not discover something absolutely clear and definite as to what the Cistercian vocation was all about. . . .

As I was laying aside the *Directory* to take up another small volume of pidgin English, someone knocked on the door.

It was a monk I had not seen before, a rather burly man with white hair and an extremely firm jaw, who introduced himself as the Master of Novices. I took another look at the determination in that jaw and said to myself: "I bet he doesn't take any nonsense from the novices, either."

But as soon as he started to talk I found that Father Master was full of a most impressive simplicity and gentleness and kindness and we began to get along together very well from that hour. He was not a man that stood on ceremony and he would have nothing to do with the notorious technique of elaborately staged humiliations which have given La Trappe a bad name in the past. By those standards he should have walked into the room and slammed the door with an insult and then asked me if I were entering the monastery in order to get away from the police.

But he just sat down and asked: "Does the silence scare you?"

I almost fell over myself in my eagerness to assure him that the silence not only did not scare me but that I was entranced with it and already felt myself to be in heaven.

"Aren't you cold here?" he asked. "Why don't you shut the window? Is that sweater warm enough?"

I assured him with consummate bravery that I was as warm as toast but he made me shut the window anyway.

Of course, what had happened was that Brother Fabian, who worked in the Guest House that year, had been feeding me with horror stories about how cold it was when you got up in the morning and went creeping down to choir with your knees knocking together and your teeth chattering so loud that you could hardly hear the prayers. So I was trying to get myself in trim for the ordeal by sitting with the windows open, without a coat on.

"Have you ever learned any Latin?" asked Father Master. I told him all about Plautus and Tacitus. He seemed satisfied.

After that we talked about many other things. Could I sing? Did I speak French? What made me want to become a Cistercian? Had I ever read anything about the Order? Had I ever read the *Life of St. Bernard* by Dom Ailbe Luddy? — and a lot of other things like that.

It was such a pleasant conversation that I was getting to be more and more unwilling to unload the big shadowy burden that still rested on my conscience, and tell this good Trappist all the things about my life before my conversion that had once made me think I could not possibly have a vocation to the priesthood. However, I finally did so in a few sentences.

"How long is it since you were baptized" said Father Master.

"Three years, Father."

He did not seem to be disturbed. He just said that he liked the way I had told him all that there was to be told, and that he would consult Father Abbot about it. And that was all.

I was still half-expecting to be called down for a cross-examination by the First Superior, but that never came. The Fat Boy from Buffalo and I waxed floors for the next couple of days, and went down to church and knelt at benches in front of St. Joseph's altar while the monks chanted the Office, and then came back to the Guest House to eat our scrambled eggs and cheese and milk. At what Brother Fabian would have described as our "last meal" he slipped us each a bar of Nestle's chocolate, and afterwards whispered to me:

"Tom, I think you are going to be a very disappointed with what you see on the table when you go into the refectory this evening. . . ."

That evening? It was the Feast of St. Lucy and a Saturday. I went back to the room and nibbled on the chocolate and copied out a poem I had just written by way of a farewell to Bob Lax and Mark Van Doren. Father Joachim came in and hid his face behind his hands to laugh when I told him what I was doing.

"*A poem?*" he said, and hastened out of the room.

He had come to get me to wax the floors some more, so presently the Fat Boy from Buffalo and I were on our knees again in the hall, but not for long. Father Master came up the stairs and told us to get our things together and follow him.

So we put on our coats and got our bags and started downstairs, leaving Father Joachim to finish waxing the floor by himself.

The noise of our footsteps resounded in the great stairwell. Down at the bottom of the flight, by the door, under the sign that said "God Alone" there were half a dozen local farmers standing around with their hats in their hands. They were waiting to go to confession. It was a kind of an anonymous, abstract delegation bidding us farewell in the name of civil society. As I passed one of them, a solemn polite old man with a four days' growth of beard, I suddenly got a somewhat melodramatic impulse and leaned over towards him whispering:

"Pray for me."

He nodded gravely that he was willing to do that, and the door closed behind us leaving me with the sense that my last act as a layman in the world still smacked of the old Thomas Merton who had gone around showing off all over two different continents.

(*The Seven Storey Mountain*, pp. 372–377)

Thomas Merton: Is It the Name of an Enemy?

By this time I should have been delivered of any problems about my true identity. I had already made my simple profession. And my vows should have divested me of the last shreds of any special identity.

But then there was this shadow, this double, this writer who had followed me into the cloister.

He is still on my track. He rides my shoulders, sometimes, like the old man of the sea. I cannot lose him. He still wears the name of Thomas Merton. Is it the name of an enemy?

He is supposed to be dead.

But he stands and meets me in the doorway of all my prayers, and follows me into church. He kneels with me behind the pillar, the Judas, and talks to me all the time in my ear.

He is a businessman. He is full of ideas. He breathes notions and new schemes. He generates books in the silence that ought to be sweet with the infinitely productive darkness of contemplation. And the worst of it is, he has my superiors on his side. They won't kick him out. I can't get rid of him. Maybe in the end he will kill me, he will drink my blood.

Nobody seems to understand that one of us has got to die.

Sometimes I am mortally afraid. There are the days when there seems to be nothing left of my vocation — my contemplative vocation — but a few ashes. And everybody calmly tells me: "Writing is your vocation."

And there he stands and bars my way to liberty. I am bound to the earth, in his Egyptian bondage of contracts, reviews, page proofs, and all the plans for books and articles that I am saddled with.

When I first began to get ideas about writing, I told them to Father Master and Father Abbot with what I thought was "simplicity." I thought I was just "being open with my superiors." In a way, I suppose I was.

But it was not long before they got the idea that I ought to be put to work translating things, writing things.

It is strange. The Trappists have sometimes been definite, even exaggerated, in their opposition to intellectual work in the past. That was one of the big battle cries of De Rancé. He had a kind of detestation for monkish dilettantes and he took up arms against the whole Benedictine congregation of Saint Maur in a more or less quixotic battle that ended in a reconciliation scene between De Rancé and the great Dom Mabillon that reads like Oliver Goldsmith. In the eighteenth and nineteenth centuries, it was considered a kind of monastic sin for a Trappist to read anything but Scripture and the lives of the saints: and I mean those lives that are a chain of fantastic miracles interspersed with pious platitudes. It was considered a matter worthy of suspicion if a monk developed too lively an interest in the Fathers of the Church.

But at Gethsemani I had walked into a far different kind of a situation.

In the first place, I entered a house that was seething with an energy and a growth that it had not known for ninety years. After nearly a century of struggle and obscurity, Gethsemani was suddenly turning into a very prominent and vital force in the Cistercian order and the Catholic Church in America. The house was crowded with postulants and novices. There was no longer any room to hold them all. In fact, on the Feast of St. Joseph, 1944, when I made my simple profession, Father Abbot read out the names of those who had been chosen for the first daughterhouse of Gethsemani. Two days later, on the Feast of St. Benedict, the colony left for Georgia and took up its abode in a barn thirty miles from Atlanta, chanting the psalms in a hayloft. By the time this is printed there will have been another Cistercian monastery in Utah and another in New Mexico, and still another planned for the deep south.

This material growth of Gethsemani is part of a vaster movement of spiritual vitality that is working throughout the whole Order all over the world. And one of the things it has produced has been a certain amount of Cistercian literature.

That there should be six Cistercian monasteries in the United States and a convent of nuns soon to come: that there should also be new foundation in Ireland and Scotland, all this means a demand for books in English about Cistercian life and the spirituality of the Order and its history.

But besides that, Gethsemani has grown into a sort of a furnace of apostolic fire. Every weekend, during the summer, the Guest House is crowded with retreatants who pray and fight the flies and wipe the sweat out of their eyes and listen to the monks chanting the office and hear sermons in the library and eat cheese that Brother Kevin makes down in the moist shadows of the cellar that is propitious for that kind of thing. And along with this retreat movement, Gethsemani has been publishing a lot of pamphlets.

There is a whole rack of them in the lobby of the Guest House. Blue and yellow and pink and green and grey, with fancy printing on the covers or plain printing — some of them even with pictures — the pamphlets bear the legend: "A Trappist says . . ." "A Trappist declares . . ." "A Trappist implores . . ." "A Trappist asserts . . ." And what does a Trappist say, declare, implore, assert? He says things like this: It is time you changed your way of looking at things. Why don't you get busy and go to confession? After death: what? and things like that. These Trappists, they have something to tell laymen and laywomen, married men and single men, old men and young men, men in the army and men who have just come out of the army and men who are too crippled up to get into the army. They have a word of advice for nuns, and more than a word for priests. They have something to say about how to build a home, and about how to go through four years of college without getting too badly knocked about, spiritually, in the process.

And one of the pamphlets even has something to say abut the Contemplative Life.

So it is not hard to see that this is a situation in which my double, my shadow, my enemy, Thomas Merton, the old man of the sea, has things in his favor. If he suggests books about the Order, his suggestions are heard. If he thinks up poems to be printed and published, his thoughts are listened to. There seems to be no reason why he should not write for magazines. . . .

At the beginning of 1944 when I was getting near the time for simple profession, I wrote a poem to Saint Agnes on her feast in January, and when I had finished it my feeling was that I did not care if I never wrote another poem as long as I lived.

At the end of the year, when *Thirty Poems* were printed, I still felt the same way, and more so.

So when Lax came down again for another Christmas, and told me I should be writing more poems, I did not argue about it. But in my own heart I did not think it was God's will. And Dom Vital, my confessor, did not think so either.

Then one day — the Feast of the Conversion of Saint Paul, 1945 — I went to Father Abbot for direction, and without my even thinking of the subject, or mentioning it, he suddenly said to me:

"I want you to go on writing poems."

(The Seven Storey Mountain, pp. 410–413)

The Christ of the Burnt Men

I hear you saying to me:

"I will give you what you desire. I will lead you into solitude. I will lead you by the way that you cannot possibly understand, because I want it to be the quickest way.

"Therefore all the things around you will be armed against you, to deny you, to hurt you, to give you pain, and therefore to reduce you to solitude.

"Because of their enmity, you will soon be left alone. They will cast you out and forsake you and reject you and you will be alone.

"Everything that touches you shall burn you, and you will draw your hand away in pain, until you have withdrawn yourself from all things. Then you will be all alone.

"Everything that can be desired will sear you, and brand you with a cautery, and you will fly from it in pain, to be alone. Every created joy will only come to you as pain, and you will die to all joy and be left alone. All the good things that other people love and desire and seek will come to you, but only as murderers to cut you off from the world and its occupations.

"You will be praised, and it will be like burning at the stake. You will be loved, and it will murder your heart and drive you into the desert.

"You will have gifts, and they will break you with their burden. You will have pleasures of prayer, and they will sicken you and you will fly from them.

"And when you have been praised a little and loved a little I will take away all your gifts and all your love and all your praise and you will be utterly forgotten and abandoned and you will be nothing, a dead thing, a rejection. And in that day you shall begin to possess the solitude you have so long desired. And your solitude will bear immense fruit in the souls of men you will never see on earth.

"Do not ask when it will be or where it will be or how it will be: On a mountain or in a prison, in a desert or in a concentration camp or in a hospital or at Gethsemani. It does not matter. So do not ask me because I am not going to tell you. You will not know until you are in it.

"But you shall taste the true solitude of my anguish and my poverty and I shall lead you into the high places of my joy and you shall die in me and find all things in my mercy which has created you for this end and brought you from Prades to Bermuda to St. Antonin to Oakham to London to Cambridge to Rome to New York to Columbia to Corpus Christi to St. Bonaventure to the Cistercian Abbey of the poor men who labor in Gethsemani:

"That you may become the brother of God and learn to know the Christ of the burnt men."

(*The Seven Storey Mountain*, pp. 422–423)

They Were Mine and I Theirs

In Louisville, at the corner of Fourth and Walnut [now Muhammad Ali], in the center of the shopping district, I was suddenly overwhelmed with the realization that I loved all those people, that they were mine and I theirs, that we could not be alien to one another even though we were total strangers. It was like awaking from a dream of separateness, of spurious self-isolation, in a special world, the world of renunciation and supposed holiness. The whole illusion of a separate holy existence is a dream. . . .

This sense of liberation from an illusory difference was such a relief and such a joy to me that I almost laughed out loud. And I suppose my happiness could have taken form in the words: "Thank God, thank God that I *am* like other men, that I am only a man among others." To think that for sixteen or seventeen years I have been taking seriously this pure illusion. . . .

It is a glorious destiny to be a member of the human race. . . . Now I realize what we all are. And if only everybody could realize this! But it cannot be explained. There is no way of telling people that they are all walking around shining like the sun.

. . . My solitude is not my own, for I see now how much it belongs to them — and that I have a responsibility for it in their regard, not just in my own. It is because I am one with them that I owe it to them to be alone, and where I am alone they are not "they" but my own self. There are no strangers.

Then it was as if I suddenly saw the secret beauty of their hearts, the depths of their hearts where neither sin nor desire nor self-knowledge can reach, the core of their reality, the person that each one is in God's eyes. If only they could all see themselves as they really *are*. If only we could see each other that way all the time. There would be no more war, no more hatred, no more cruelty, no more greed. . . . I suppose the big problem would be that we would fall down and worship each other. But this cannot be *seen*, only believed and "understood" by a peculiar gift.

. . . At the center of our being is a point of nothingness which is untouched by sin and by illusions, a point of pure truth, a point or spark which belongs entirely to God, which is never at our disposal, from which God disposes our lives, which is inaccessible to the fantasies of our own mind or the brutalities of our own will. This little point of nothingness and of *absolute poverty* is the pure glory of God in us. It is so to speak His name written in us, as our poverty, as our indigence, as our dependence, as our sonship. It is like a pure diamond, blazing with the invisible light of heaven. It is in everybody, and if we could see it we would see these billions of points of light coming together in the face and blaze of a sun that would make all the darkness and cruelty of life vanish completely. . . . I have no program for this seeing. It is only given. But the gate of heaven is everywhere.

(*Conjectures of a Guilty Bystander*, pp. 140–142)

Everybody Was Proverb

It is a simple enough story but obviously I do not tell it to people — you are the fourth who knows it, and there seems to be no point in a false discretion that might restrain me from telling you since it is clear that we have so very much in common. One night [February 28, 1958] I dreamt that I was sitting with a very young Jewish girl of fourteen or fifteen, and that she suddenly manifested a very deep affection for me and embraced me so that I was moved to the depths of my soul. I learned that her name was "Proverb," which I thought very simple and beautiful. And also I thought, "She is of the race of Saint Anne." I spoke to her of her name, and she did not seem to be proud of it, because it seemed rather the other young girls mocked her for it. But I told her that it was a very beautiful name, and there the dream ended. A few days later when I happened to be in a nearby city [March 18, Louisville], which is very rare for us, I was walking alone in the crowded street and suddenly saw that everybody was Proverb and that in all of them shone her extraordinary beauty and purity and shyness, even though they did not know who they were and were perhaps ashamed of their names — because they were mocked on account of them. And they did not know their real identity as the Child so dear to God who, from before the beginning, was playing in His sight all days, playing in the world. Thus you are initiated into the scandalous secret of a monk who is in love with a girl, and a Jew at that! One cannot expect much from monks these days. The heroic asceticism of the past is no more.

(Letter to Boris Pasternak
Pasternak-Merton Letters, p. 12)

I Have no Idea Where I am Going

My Lord God, I have no idea where I am going. I do not see the road ahead of me. I cannot know for certain where it will end. Nor do I really know myself, and the fact that I think I am following your will does not mean that I am actually doing so. But I believe that the desire to please you does in fact please you. And I hope I have that desire in all that I am doing. I hope that I will never do anything apart from that desire. And I know that if I do this you will lead me by the right road, though I may know nothing about it. Therefore I will trust you always though I may seem to be lost and in the shadow of death. I will not fear, for you are ever with me, and you will never leave me to face my perils alone.

(*Thoughts in Solitude*, p. 81)

O Holy Queen of Souls and Refuge of Sinners

Glorious Mother of God, shall I ever again distrust you, or your God, before whose throne you are irresistible in your intercession? Shall I ever turn my eyes from your hands and from your face and from your eyes? Shall I ever look anywhere else but in the face of your love, to find out true counsel, and to know my way, in all the days and all the moments of my life?

As you have dealt with me, Lady, deal also with all my millions of brothers who live in the same misery that I knew then: lead them in spite of themselves and guide them by your tremendous influence, O Holy Queen of souls and refuge of sinners, and bring them to your Christ the way you brought me. *Illos tuos misericordes oculos ad nos converte, et Jesum, benedictum fructum ventris tui, nobis ostende,* Show us your Christ, Lady, after this our exile, yes: but show him to us also now, show him to us here, while we are still wanderers.

(*The Seven Storey Mountain*, p. 130)

Friends and More

In the course of his writings Thomas Merton has given us some candid insights into the men, well known and less so, who exercised a formative influence in his life. Reading these not only gives us insight into these men — who will certainly be read in a different light once we have listened to what Merton has had to say — but also into Merton himself and his thinking. Some of them, like Gandhi, first spoke to him quite early in life, yet their influence perdured and in some instances came to full blossom only much later on. The few influences Merton speaks of here present a colorful array. And many, many more could be added to this procession. I have chosen these passages because they bear most directly on the thought of Merton as it is found in other passages in this anthology.

Mahatma Gandhi

One of the most significant facts about the life and vocation of Gandhi was his discovery of the East through the West. Like so many others of India, Gandhi received a completely Western education as a young man. He had to a great extent renounced the beliefs, the traditions, the habits of thought, of India. He spoke, thought, and acted like an Englishman, except of course that an Englishman was precisely what he could never, by any miracle, become. He was an alienated Asian whose sole function in life was to be perfectly English without being English at all: to prove the superiority of the West by betraying his own heritage and his own self, thinking as a white man without ceasing to be "a Nigger." The beauty of this (at least in Western minds) was that it showed Western culture to be a pearl of such great price that one could reasonably sell the whole of Asia in order to acquire it, even though the acquisition was not that of a new being, or even of a new identity, but only of a new suit.

Gandhi was unusual in this. Instead of being fooled by the Western costume, and instead of being persuaded that the West had something good about it that was good not because it was Western but because it was also Eastern: that is to say, it was *universal*. So he turned his face and his heart once again to India, and saw what was really there. It was through his acquaintance with writers like Tolstoy and Thoreau, and then his reading of the New Testament, that Gandhi discovered his own tradition and his Hindu *dharma* (religion, duty). More than a tradition, more than a wisdom handed down in books or celebrated in temples, Gandhi discovered India in discovering himself. Hence it is very important indeed to understand Gandhi's political life, and particularly his non-violence, in the light of this radical discovery from which everything else received its meaning. Gandhi's dedicated struggle for Indian freedom and his insistence on non-violent means in the struggle — both resulted from his new understanding of India and of himself after his contact with a *universally valid* spiritual tradition which he saw to be common to both East and West.

The Christianity, the spiritual and religious humanism, of the West opened his eyes to forces of wisdom and of love which were closer to his own heart because they were expressed in the symbols and philosophic language of his own people, and they could be used immediately to awaken this sleeping and enslaved people to an awareness of its own identity and of its historic vocation. He neither accepted Christianity nor rejected it; he took all that he found in Christian thought that seemed relevant to him as a Hindu. The rest was, at least for the time being, of merely external interest.

Here was no syncretism and no indifferentism. Gandhi had the deepest respect for Christianity, for Christ and the Gospel. In following his way of *satyagraha* he believed he was following the Law of Christ, and it would be difficult to prove that this belief was entirely mistaken — or that it was in any degree insincere.

One of the great lessons of Gandhi's life remains this: through the spiritual traditions of the West he, an Indian, discovered his Indian heritage and with it his own "right mind." And in his fidelity to his own heritage and its spiritual sanity, he was able to show men of the West and of the whole world a way to recover their own "right mind" in their own tradition, thus manifesting the fact that there are certain indisputable and essential values — religious, ethical, ascetic, spiritual, and philosophical — which man had everywhere needed and which he has in the past managed to acquire, values without which he cannot live, values which are now in large measure lost to him so that, unequipped to face life in a fully human manner, he now runs the risk of destroying himself entirely. . . .

In rediscovering India and his own "right mind," Gandhi was not excavating from libraries the obscure disputed questions of Vedantic scholasticism (though he did not reject Vedanta). He was, on the contrary, identifying himself fully with the Indian people, that is to say not with the Westernized upper classes nor with the Brahmin caste, but rather with the starving masses and in particular with the outcast "untouchables," or *Harijan*.

This again is a supremely important fact, without which Gandhi's non-violence is incomprehensible. The awakening of the Indian mind in Gandhi was not simply the awakening of his own spirit to the possibilities of a distinctly Hindu form of "interior life." It was not just a question of Yoga *asanas* and Vedantic spiritual disciplines for his own perfection. Gandhi realized that *the people of India were awakening in him*. The masses who had been totally silent for thousands of years had now found a voice in him. It was not "Indian thought" or "Indian spirituality" that was stirring in him, but India herself. It was the spiritual consciousness of a people that awakened in the spirit of one person. But the message of the Indian spirit, of Indian wisdom, was not for India alone. It was for the entire world. Hence Gandhi's message was valid for India and for himself insofar as it represented *the awakening of a new world*.

Yet this renewed spiritual consciousness of India was entirely different from the totalitarian and nationalist consciousness that came alive in the West and in the East (Japan) to the point of furious and warlike vitality. The Indian mind that was awakening in Gandhi was inclusive, not exclusive. It was at once Indian and universal. It was not a mind of hate, of intolerance, of accusation, of rejection, of division. It was a mind of love, of understanding, of infinite capaciousness. Where the extreme nationalisms of Western Fascism and of Japan were symptoms of paranoid fury, exploding into alienation, division, and destruction, the spirit which Gandhi discovered in himself was reaching out to unity, love, and peace. It was a spirit which was, he believed, strong enough to heal every division.

In Gandhi's mind, non-violence was not simply a political tactic which was supremely useful and efficacious in liberating his people from foreign rule, in order that India might then concentrate on realizing its own national identity. On the contrary, the spirit of non-violence sprang from *an inner realization of spiritual unity in himself.* The whole Gandhian concept of non-violent action and *satyagraha* is incomprehensible if it is thought to be a means of achieving unity rather than as *the fruit of inner unity already achieved.* . . .

In Gandhi the voice of Asia, not the Asia of the Vedas and Sutras only, but the Asia of the hungry and silent masses, was speaking and still speaks to the whole world with a prophetic message. This message, uttered on dusty Indian roads, remains more meaningful than those specious promises that have come from the great capitols of the earth. As Father Monchanin, the French priest and scholar who became a hermit in India, declared at Gandhi's death: "When we hear the voice of Gandhi we hear the voice of his Mother [India] and of his nurse. We hear the voice of all the peasant masses bending over the rice fields of India." . . .

Sometimes the idea of non-violence is taken to be the result of a purely sentimental evasion of unpleasant Westerners with the idea that for the East (and as everyone knows, the Easterners are all "quietists" besides being "enigmatic") nothing really exists anyway. All is illusion, and suffering itself is illusion. Non-violence becomes a way of "making violence stop" by sitting down in front of it and wishing it was not there. This, together with the refusal to eat meat or to kill ants, indeed even mosquitoes, is supposedly thought to create an aura of benevolence which may effectively inhibit the violence of Englishmen (who are in any case kind to dogs, etc.) but cannot be expected to work against Nazis and Russians. So much for Western evaluations!

Gandhi knew the reality of hatred and untruth because he had felt them in his own flesh: indeed he succumbed to them when he was assassinated on January 30, 1948. Gandhi's non-violence was therefore not a sentimental evasion or denial of the reality of evil. It was a clearsighted acceptance of the necessity to use the force and the presence of evil as a fulcrum for good and for liberation.

(*Gandhi on Non-Violence*, pp. 3–11)

Mark Van Doren

Soon I was full of all the economic and pseudo-scientific jargon appropriate to a good Columbia man, and was acclimated to the new atmosphere which I found so congenial. That was true. Columbia, compared with Cambridge, was a friendly place. When you had to go to see a professor or an advisor or a dean about something, he would tell you, more or less simply, what you needed to know. The only trouble was that you usually had to wait around for about half an hour before you got a chance to see anybody. But once you did, there were no weird evasions and none of the pompous beating about the bush, mixed with subtle academic allusions and a few dull witticisms which was what you were liable to get out of almost anybody at Cambridge, where everybody cultivated some special manner of his own, and you have to expect around a university, this artificiality. For a man to be absolutely sincere with generation after generation of students requires either supernatural simplicity or, in the natural order, a kind of heroic humility. There was — and still is — one man at Columbia, or rather one among several, who was most remarkable for this kind of heroism. I mean Mark Van Doren.

The first semester I was at Columbia, just after my twentieth birthday, in the winter of 1935, Mark was giving part of the "English sequence" in one of those rooms in Hamilton Hall with windows looking out between the big columns on the wired-in track on South Field. There were twelve or fifteen people with more or less unbrushed hair, most of them with glasses, lounging around. One of them was my friend Robert Gibney.

It was a class in English literature, and it had no special bias of any kind. It was simply about what it was supposed to be about: the English literature of the eighteenth century. And in it literature was treated, not as history, not as sociology, not as economics, not as a series of case histories in psychoanalysis but, *mirabile dictu*, simply as literature.

I thought to myself, who is this excellent man Van Doren who being employed to teach literature, teaches just that: talks about writing and about books and poems and plays: does not get off on a tangent about the biographies of the poets or novelists: does not read into their poems a lot of subjective messages which were never there? Who is this man who does not have to fake and cover up a big gulf of ignorance by teaching a lot of opinions and conjectures and useless facts that belong to some other subject? Who is this who really loves what he has to teach, and does not secretly detest all literature, and abhor poetry, while pretending to be a professor of it?

That Columbia should have in it men like this who, instead of subtly destroying all literature by burying and concealing it under a mass of irrelevancies, really purified and educated the perceptions of their students by teaching them how to read a book and how to tell a good book from a bad, genuine writing from falsity and pastiche: all this gave me a deep respect for my new university.

Mark would come into the room and, without fuss, would start talking about whatever was to be talked about. Most of the time he asked questions. His questions were very good, and if you tried to answer them intelligently, you found yourself saying excellent things that you did not know you knew, and that you had not, in fact, known before. He had "educed"

— them from you by his question. His classes were literally "education" — they brought things out of you, they made your mind produce its own explicit ideas. Do not think that Mark was simply priming his students with thoughts of his own, and then making the thought stick to their minds by getting them to give it back to him as their own. Far from it. What he did have was the gift of communicating to them something of his own vital interest in things, something of his manner of approach: but the results were sometimes quite unexpected — and by that I mean good in a way that he had not anticipated, casting lights that he had not himself foreseen.

Now a man who can go for year after year — although Mark was young then and is young now — without having any time to waste in flattering and cajoling his students with any kind of fancy act, or with jokes, or with storms of temperament, or periodic tirades — whole classes spent in threats and imprecations, to disguise the fact that the professor himself has come in unprepared — one who can do without all these non-essentials both honors his vocation and makes it fruitful. Not only that, but his vocation, in return, perfects and ennobles him. And that is the way it should be, even in the natural order: how much more so in the order of grace!

Mark, I know, is no stranger to the order of grace: but considering his work as teacher merely as a mission on the natural level — I can see that Providence was using him as an instrument more directly than he realized. As far as I can see, the influence of Mark's sober and sincere intellect, with his manner of dealing with his subject with perfect honesty and objectivity and without evasions, was remotely preparing my mind to receive the good seed of scholastic philosophy. And there is nothing strange in this, for Mark himself was familiar at least with some of the modern scholastics, like Maritain and Gilson, and he was a friend of the American neo-

Thomists, Mortimer Adler and Richard McKeon, who had started out at Columbia but had had to move to Chicago, because Columbia was not ripe enough to know what to make of them.

The truth is that Mark's temper was profoundly scholastic in the sense that his clear mind looked directly for the quiddities of things, and sought being and substance under the covering of accident and appearances. And for him poetry was, indeed, a virtue of the practical intellect, and not simply a vague spilling of the emotions, wasting the soul and perfecting none of our essential powers.

It was because of this virtual scholasticism of Mark's that he would never permit himself to fall into the naive errors of those who try to read some favorite private doctrine into every poet they like of every nation and every age. And Mark abhorred the smug assurance with which second-rate left-wing critics find adumbrations of dialectical materialism in everyone who ever wrote from Homer and Shakespeare to whomever they happen to like in recent times. If the poet is to their fancy, then he is clearly seen to be preaching the class struggle. If they do not like him, then they are able to show that he was really a forefather of fascism. And all their literary heroes are revolutionary leaders, and all their favorite villains are capitalists and Nazis.

It was a very good thing for me that I ran into someone like Mark Van Doren at that particular time, because in my new reverence for Communism, I was in danger of docilely accepting any kind of stupidity, provided I thought it was something that paved the way to the Elysian fields of classless society. . . .

I have already mentioned Mark Van Doren. It would not be exactly true to say that he was a kind of nucleus around whom this concretion of friends formed itself: that would not be accurate. Not all of us took his courses, and those who did, did not do so all at the same time. And yet nevertheless our common respect for Mark's sanity and wisdom did much to make us aware of how much we ourselves had in common.

Perhaps it was for me, personally, more than for the others, that Mark's course worked in this way. I am thinking of one particular incident.

It was the fall of 1936, just at the beginning of the new school year — one of those bright, crazy days when everybody is full of ambition. It was the beginning of the year in which Pop was going to die and my own resistance would cave in under the load of pleasures and ambitions I was too weak to carry: the year in which I would be all the time getting dizzy, and in which I learned to fear the Long Island railroad as if it were some kind of monster, and to shrink from New York as if it were the wide-open mouth of some burning Aztec god.

That day, I did not foresee any of this. My veins were still bursting with the materialistic and political enthusiasms with which I had first come to Columbia and, indeed, in line with their general direction, I had signed up for courses that were more or less sociological and economic and historical. In the obscurity of the strange, half-conscious semi-conversion that had attended my retreat from Cambridge, I had tended more and more to be suspicious of literature, poetry — the things towards which my nature drew me — on the grounds that they might lead to a sort of futile estheticism, a philosophy of "escape."

This had not involved me in any depreciation of people like Mark. However, it had just seemed more important to me that I should take some history course, rather than anything that was still left of his for me to take.

So now I was climbing one of the crowded stairways in Hamilton Hall to the room where I thought this history course was to be given. I looked into the room. The second row was filled with the unbrushed heads of those who every day at

noon sat in the *Jester* editorial offices and threw paper air-
planes around the room or drew pictures on the walls.

Taller than them all, and more serious, with a long face, like
a horse, and a great mane of black hair on top of it, Bob Lax
meditated on some incomprehensible woe, and waited for
someone to come in and begin to talk to them. It was when I
had taken off my coat and put down my load of books that I
found out that this was not the class I was supposed to be
taking, but Van Doren's course on Shakespeare.

So I got up to go out. But when I got to the door I turned
around again and went back and sat down where I had been,
and stayed there. Later I went and changed everything with
the registrar, so I remained in that class for the rest of the year.

It was the best course I ever had in college. And it did me
the most good, in many different ways. It was the only place
where I ever heard anything really sensible said about any of
the things that were really fundamental — life, death, time,
love, sorrow, fear, wisdom, suffering, eternity. A course in
literature should never be a course in economics or philosophy
or sociology or psychology: and I have explained how it was
one of Marks' great virtues that he did not make it so. Nevertheless, the material of literature and especially of drama is
chiefly human acts — that is, free acts, moral acts. And, as a
matter of fact, literature, drama, poetry, make certain statements about these acts that can be made in no other way. That
is precisely why you will miss all the deepest meaning of
Shakespeare, Dante, and the rest if you reduce their vital and
creative statements about life and men to the dry, matter-of-
fact terms of history, or ethics, or some other science. They
belong to a different order.

Nevertheless, the great power of something like *Hamlet,
Coriolanus*, or the *Purgatorio* or Donne's *Holy Sonnets* lies precisely in the fact that they are a kind of commentary on ethics
and psychology and even metaphysics, even theology. Or,

sometimes, it is the other way 'round, and those sciences can serve as a commentary on these other realities, which we call plays, poems.

All that year we were, in fact, talking about the deepest springs of human desire and hope and fear; we were considering all the most important realities, not indeed in terms of something alien to Shakespeare and to poetry, but precisely in his own terms, with occasional intuitions of another order. And, as I have said, Mark's balanced and sensitive and clear way of seeing things, at once simple and yet capable of subtlety, being fundamentally scholastic, though not necessarily and explicitly Christian, presented these things in ways that made them live within us, and with a life that was healthy and permanent and productive. This class was one of the few things that could persuade me to get on the train and go to Columbia at all. It was, that year, my only health, until I came across and read the Gilson book.

(*The Seven Storey Mountain*, pp. 138–141, 178–180)

Robert Lax

I began to discover who Bob Lax was, and that in him was a combination of Mark's [Van Doren] clarity and my confusion and misery — and a lot more besides that was his own.

To name Robert Lax in another way, he was a kind of combination of Hamlet and Elias. A potential prophet, but without rage. A king, but a Jew, too. A mind full of tremendous and subtle intuitions, and every day he found less and less to say about them, and resigned himself to being inarticulate. In his hesitations, though without embarrassment or nervousness at all, he would often curl his long legs all around a chair, in seven different ways, while he was trying to find a word with which to begin. He talked best sitting on the floor.

And the secret of his constant solidity I think has always been a kind of natural, instinctive spirituality, a kind of inborn direction to the living God. Lax has always been afraid he was in a blind alley, and half aware that, after all, it might not be a blind alley, but God, infinity.

He had a mind naturally disposed, from the very cradle, to a kind of affinity for Job and St. John of the Cross. And I now know that he was born so much of a contemplative that he will probably never be able to find out how much.

To sum it up, even the people who have always thought he was "too impractical" have always tended to venerate him — in the way people who value material security unconsciously venerate people who do not fear insecurity.

In those days one of the things we had most in common, although perhaps we did not talk about it so much, was the abyss that walked around in front of our feet everywhere we went, and kept making us dizzy and afraid of trains and high buildings. For some reason, Lax developed an implicit trust in all my notions about what was good and bad for mental and physical health, perhaps because I was always very definite in my likes and dislikes. I am afraid it did not do him too much good, though. For even though I had my imaginary abyss, which broadened immeasurably and became ten times dizzier when I had a hangover, my ideas often tended to some particular place where we would hear this particular band and drink this special drink until the place folded up at four o'clock in the morning.

(*The Seven Storey Mountain*, p. 181)

Daniel Walsh

This man was Daniel Walsh, about whom I had heard a great deal from Lax and Gerdy. Gerdy had taken his course on St. Thomas Aquinas in the graduate school of Philosophy: and now as the new school year began, my attention centered upon this one course. It had nothing directly to do with my preparation for the exams for the M.A. degree in January. By now degrees and everything else to do with a university career had become very unimportant in comparison with the one big thing that occupied my mind and all my desire.

I registered for the course, and Dan Walsh turned out to be another one of those destined in a providential way to shape and direct my vocation. For it was he who pointed out my way to the place where I now am.

When I was writing about Columbia and its professors, I was not thinking of Dan Walsh; and he really did not belong to Columbia at all. He was on the faculty of the Sacred Heart College at Manhattanville, and came to Columbia twice a week to lecture on St. Thomas and Duns Scotus. His class was a small one and was, as far as Columbia was concerned, pretty much of an academic bypath. And that was in a sense an additional recommendation — it was off that broad and noisy highway of pragmatism which leads between its banks of artificial flowers to the gates of despair.

Walsh himself had nothing of the supercilious self-assurance of the ordinary professor: he did not need this frail and artificial armor for his own insufficiency. He did not need to hide behind tricks and vanities any more than Mark Van Doren did; he never even needed to be brilliant. In this smiling simplicity he used to efface himself entirely in the solid and powerful mind of St. Thomas. Whatever brilliance he allowed himself to show forth in his lectures was all thrown back upon its source, the Angel of the Schools.

Dan Walsh had been a student and collaborator of Gilson's and knew Gilson and Maritain well. In fact, later on he introduced me to Maritain at the Catholic Book Club, where this most saintly philosopher had been giving a talk on Catholic Action. . . .

But Dan himself had caught a tremendous amount of this simplicity and gentleness and godliness too: and perhaps the impression that he made was all the more forceful because his square jaw had a kind of potential toughness about it. Yet no: there he sat, this little, stocky man, who had something of the appearance of a goodnatured prize fighter, smiling and talking with the most childlike delight and cherubic simplicity about the *Summa Theologica*.

His voice was low and, as he spoke, he half apologetically searched the faces of his hearers for signs of understanding and, when he found it, he seemed surprised and delighted.

I very quickly made friends with him, and told him all about my thesis and the ideas I was trying to work with, and he was very pleased. And one of the things he sensed at once was something that I was far from being able to realize: but it was that the bent of my mind was essentially "Augustinian." I had not yet followed Bramachari's advice to read St. Augustine and I did not take Dan's evaluation of my ideas as having all the directive force that was potentially in it — for it did not even come clothed in suggestion or advice.

Of course, to be called "Augustinian" by a Thomist might not in every case be a compliment. But coming from Dan Walsh, who was a true Catholic philosopher, it was a compliment indeed.

For he, like Gilson, had the most rare and admirable virtue of being able to rise above the petty differences of schools and systems, and seeing Catholic philosophy in its wholeness, in its variegated unity, and in its true Catholicity. In other words, he was able to study St. Thomas and St. Bonaventure and

Duns Scotus side by side, and to see them as complementing and reinforcing one another, as throwing diverse and individual light on the same truths from different points of view, and thus he avoided the evil of narrowing and restricting Catholic philosophy and theology to a single school, to a single attitude, a single system.

I pray to God that there may be raised up more like him in the Church and in our universities, because there is something stifling and intellectually deadening about textbooks that confine themselves to giving a superficial survey of the field of philosophy according to Thomist principles and then discard all the rest in a few controversial objections. Indeed, I think it a great shame and a danger of no small proportions that Catholic philosophers should be trained in division against one another, and brought up to the bitterness and smallness of controversy: because this is bound to narrow their views and dry up the unction that should vivify all philosophy in their souls.

(*The Seven Storey Mountain*, pp. 218–220)

Jacques Maritain

I only spoke a few conventional words to Maritain, but the impression you got from this gentle, stooping Frenchman with much grey hair, was one of tremendous kindness and simplicity and godliness. And that was enough: you did not need to talk to him. I came away feeling very comforted that there was such a person in the world, and confident that he would include me in some way in his prayers.

(*The Seven Storey Mountain*, p. 219)

The eminent Japanese philosopher Kitaro Nishida (1870–1945) did for Zen Buddhism a work analogous to that of Jacques Maritain in Catholic philosophy; he constructed, within his own mystical tradition, and on the basis of its traditional and spiritual intuitions, a philosophy which at the same time speaks to modern — even Western — man, and remains open to the highest wisdom which it seeks in union with God.

(*Thomas Merton on Zen*, p. 117)

Ernesto Cardenal

Let's suppose this place [Gethsemani] is closed tomorrow. In twelve hours I'm in Nicaragua on that island [Solentiname] with this ex-novice of mine [Cardenal], the married couple, the ten peasant families, and some intellectuals of Nicaragua, which is where I've been wanting to go for fifteen years. I would continue to live the way I'm living now. They've asked me to come down there. . . .

Yes, I'm choosing community as the place where Christ is present and acting. And he has shown this to me by the fact that these are my friends. These are people I know. We have already discussed it and we feel it's a place where we could really do something. . . . We're mostly writers and poets. We understand things very much the same way.

Let me go back into the vocation of this man who came here, the poet from Nicaragua, Ernesto Cardenal. I remember distinctly when his application came in. It was an average application from a Latin American. We don't quickly accept people from a long distance away: they come all the way here and in three days the whole thing blows and you have to pay their fare back home! I knew that the abbot didn't particularly want to take him, but something just said, "This is a great guy!" He came, and we got along fine.

Today he's one of the best poets in Latin America. He's a remarkable person and extremely humble. He's had an immense influence. He publishes in a lot of Latin American journals and is very well received, one of the few people who are respected as Catholics and as intellectuals from one end of the country to the other. He puts out a little mimeographed paper every two or three months and sends it around to various people. They like it. They see it as something good going on in this monastery. With no effort on his part, the paper gets quoted in intellectual magazines. He's simply being himself and there's spontaneous radiation.

(*The Springs of Contemplation*, pp. 243–245)

Daisetz Suzuki

Incidentally, I was very happy and edified, surprised and encouraged one time when I got into a dialogue with the Zen Buddhist Daisetz Suzuki, a marvelous old man. He is highly respected all over the world, an international figure and a great contemplative. We got into a written dialogue about contemplative life and Zen, which led to some discussion about original sin and the Fall.

I developed the idea in the way the Fathers of the Church did. . . .

What struck me about Suzuki was that he came back with some fantastic ideas which could have come from Saint Augustine, whom he's never read. Or from the other early Christian writers. It was exactly like that; Suzuki says that Zen brings us back into this realm of straight being, away from the realm of mere existence and activity. And that the purpose of Zen, which we mentioned here in passing, is simply to get us detached from the notion that passing things are definitive.

(The Springs of Contemplation, pp. 259–261)

John C. H. Wu

Dr. John C. H. Wu is in a uniquely favorable position to interpret Zen for the West. He has given courses on Zen in Chinese and in American universities An eminent jurist and diplomat, a Chinese convert to Catholicism, a scholar but also a man of profoundly humorous simplicity and spiritual freedom, he is able to write of Buddhism not from hearsay or study alone, but from within. Dr. Wu is not afraid to admit that he brought Zen, Taoism and Confucianism with him into Christianity. In fact in his well-known Chinese translation of the New Testament he opens the Gospel of St. John with the words, "In the beginning was the Tao."

He nowhere feels himself obliged to pretend that Zen causes him to have dizzy spells or palpitations of the heart. Nor does he attempt the complex and frustrating task of trying to conciliate Zen insights with Christian doctrine. He simply takes hold of Zen and presents it without comment. Anyone who has any familiarity with Zen will immediately admit that this is the only way to talk about it. To approach the subject with an intellectual or theological chip on the shoulder would end only in confusion. The truth of the matter is that you can hardly set Christianity and Zen side by side and compare them. This would almost be like trying to compare mathematics and tennis. And if you are writing a book on tennis which might conceivably be read by many mathematicians, there is little point in bringing mathematics into the discussion — but to stick to the tennis. That is what Dr. Wu has done with Zen.

On the other hand, Zen is deliberatively cryptic and disconcerting. It seems to say the most outrageous things about the life of the spirit. It seems to jolt even the Buddhist mind out of its familiar thought routines and devout imaginings, and no doubt it will be even more shocking to those whose religious outlook is remote from Buddhism. Zen can sound, at times, frankly and avowedly irreligious. And it is, in the sense that it makes a direct attack on formalism and myth, and regards conventional religiosity as a hindrance to mature religious development. On the other hand, in what sense is Zen, as such, "religious" at all? Yet where do we ever find "pure Zen" dissociated from a religious and cultural matrix of some sort? Some of the Zen Masters were iconoclasts. But the life of an ordinary Zen temple is full of Buddhist piety and ritual, and some Zen literature abounds in devotionalism and in conventional Buddhist religious concepts. The Zen of D. T. Suzuki is completely free from all this. But can it be called "typical"? One of the advantages of Dr. Wu's Christian treatment is that he, too, is able to see Zen apart from this accidental setting. It is like seeing the mystical doctrine of St. John of the Cross apart from the somewhat irrelevant backdrop of Spanish baroque. However, the whole study of Zen can bristle with questions like these, and when the well-meaning inquirer receives answers to his questions, then hundreds of other questions arise to take the place of the two or three that have been "answered."

(*Thomas Merton on Zen*, pp. 91–92)

First of All a Poet

Thomas Merton is "first of all a poet" in the sense that his first published volume was indeed a book of poetry, a very slim volume, *Thirty Poems*, published by a man who in time would become his close friend, one of his literary executors, and the publisher of the thick volume of Merton's *Collected Poems*: J Laughlin. But it is also true that Merton as a writer thought of himself first of all as a poet. He had a deeply poetic spirit. He struggled with this literary genre all his life. It promised more than others to provide him with the means of giving expression to some of his deeper experiences. In this he followed in the footsteps of some of the great mystics, especially John of the Cross, who had such a marked influence upon him. Yet in the end it also seems to have failed him.

Few of Merton's poems can lay claim to having attained anything approaching true greatness. But to completely neglect them would be to neglect an important part of Thomas Merton and to miss the opportunity for sharing some significant moments in his life as well as to miss some important insights into the man and the monk.

We include in this brief section some of his early and more apparently religious poems. The most beautiful and most significant is the one he wrote on the occasion of his brother's death. We will leave to a later section the sometimes more powerful poetry of the social critic that belongs to a later period in his journey.

For My Brother:
Reported Missing in Action, 1943

Sweet brother, if I do not sleep
My eyes are flowers for your tomb;
And if I cannot eat my bread,
My fasts shall live like willows where you died.
If in the heat I find no water for my thirst,
My thirst shall turn to springs for you, poor traveler.

Where, in what desolate and smokey country,
Lies your poor body, lost and dead?
And in what landscape of disaster
Has your unhappy spirit lost its road?

Come, in my labor find a resting place
And in my sorrows lay your head,
Or rather take my life and blood
And buy yourself a better bed —
Or take my breath and take my death
And buy yourself a better rest.

When all the men of war are shot
And flags have fallen into dust,
Your cross and mine shall tell men still
Christ died on each, for both of us.

For in the wreckage of your April Christ lies slain,
And Christ weeps in the ruins of my spring:
The money of Whose tears shall fall
Into your weak and friendless hand,
And buy you back to your own land:
The silence of Whose tears shall fall

Like bells upon your alien tomb.
Hear them and come: they call you home.

(*The Seven Storey Mountain*, p. 404)

Hymn of Not Much Praise for New York City

When the windows of the West Side clash like cymbals in the
    setting sunlight,
And when wind wails amid the East Side aerials,
And when, both north and south of Thirty-fourth Street,
In all the dizzy buildings,
The elevators clack their teeth and rattle the bars of
    their cages,
Then children of the city,
Leaving the monkey-houses of their office-buildings
    and apartments,
With the greatest difficulty open their mouths, and sing:

"Queen among the cities of the Earth: New York!
Rich as a cake, common as a doughnut,
Expensive as a fur and crazy as cocaine,
We love to hear you shake
Your big face like a shining bank
Letting the mad world know you're full of dimes!

"This is your night to make maracas out of all that metal
    money
Paris is in the prison-house, and London dies of cancer.

This is the time for you to whirl,
Queen of our hopped-up peace,
And let the excitement of your somewhat crippled congas

Supersede the waltzes of more shining
Capitals that have been bombed.

"Meanwhile we, your children,
weeping in our seasick zoo of windows while you dance,
Will gobble aspirins,
And try to keep our cage from caving in.
All the while our minds will fill with these petitions,
Flowering quietly in between our gongs of pulse.
These will have to serve as prayers:

" 'O lock us in the safe jails of thy movies!
Confine us to the semiprivate wards and white asylums
Of the unbearable cocktail parties, O New York!
Sentence us for life to the penitentiaries of thy bars and
          nightclubs,
And leave us stupefied forever by the blue, objective lights
That fill the pale infirmaries of thy restaurants,
And the clinics of thy schools and offices,
And the operating-rooms of thy dance-halls.

" 'But never give us any explanation, even when we ask,
Why all our food tastes of iodoform,
And even the freshest flowers smell of funerals.
No, never let us look about us long enough to wonder
which of the rich men, shivering in the overheated office,
And which of the poor men, sleeping face-down on
          the *Daily Mirror*,
Are still alive, and which are dead.' "

(*Collected Poems*, pp. 19ff)

Aubade — Harlem
for Baroness C. de Hueck

Across the cages of the keyless aviaries,
The lines and wires, the gallows of the broken kites,
Crucify, against the fearful light,
The ragged dresses of the little children.
Soon, in the sterile jungles of the x and ladders
The bleeding sun, a bird of prey, will terrify the poor,
These will forget the unbelievable moon.

But in the cells of whiter buildings,
Where the glass dawn is brighter than the knives of surgeons,
Paler than alcohol or ether, shinier than money,
The white men's wives, like Pilate's,
Cry in peril of their frozen dreams:

"Daylight has driven iron spikes,
Into the flesh of Jesus' hands and feet:
Four flowers of blood have nailed Him to the walls
        of Harlem."

Along the white halls of the clinics and the hospitals
Pilate evaporates with a cry:
They have cut down two hundred Judases,
Hanged by the neck in the opera houses and the museum.

Across the cages of the keyless aviaries,
The lines and wires, the gallows of the broken kites,
Crucify, against the fearful light,
The ragged dresses of the little children.

(*Collected Poems*, pp. 82f)

The Strife Between the Poet and Ambition

Money and fame break in the room
And find the poet all alone.
They lock the door, so he won't run,
And turn the radio full-on
And beat the poor dope like a drum.

"Better sing your snatch of song
Before that ostrich voice is dumb,
Better hit your share of gong
Before the sounding brass is mum:
Tomorrow, tomorrow Death will come
And find you sitting dumb and senseless
With your epics unbegun,
And take away your pens and pencils—

There'll be no sculptures on your tomb
And other bards will occupy
Your seven-fifty sitting room."
"Pardon, sirs, my penny face
Bowed to your dollar presences,
Curtsying to Famous Verse,
Flattering wealth with smiles and smirks,
Choking down my hopeless tears!
For someone stole my crate of birds,
And busted up the music box
In which I kept my market flocks
Of bull-ideas and mental bears
And my poetic pocketfox,
My case of literary deers,
My eagle-vans to bat the airs!
They broke the cages and let go
My aviary of metric birds,

And all the diction in my zoo
Was let out by the amateurs!
The fishpond of my Friday words
Is fished out by the days and years.
My whole menagerie of verse
Is ruined by these sly monsieurs!"

The days and years run down the beach
And throw his ideas in the air
And wind his similes up to pitch
And bat his verses out of reach.
He mopes along the empty shore
With gullcries in his windfilled ear.
The hours and minutes, playing catch
With every image they can snatch,
Bat his metaphors to the birds
And cheer him with these bullying words:
"Better sing your snatch of song
Before that ostrich voice is dumb:
Better whack your share of gong
Before the sounding brass is mum:
Tomorrow, tomorrow Death will come
And find your epics unbegun:
There'll be no statues on your tomb,
And other bards will occupy
Your seven-fifty sitting room!"

(*Collected Poems*, pp. 10ff)

Elias — Variations on a Theme

The free man is not alone as busy men are
But as birds are. The free man sings

Alone as universes do. Built
Upon his own inscrutable pattern
Clear, unmistakable, not invented by himself alone
Or for himself, but for the universe also.

Nor does he make it his business to be recognized
Or care to have himself found out
As if some special subterfuge were needed
To get himself known for who he is.

The free man does not float
On the tides of his own expedition
Nor is he sent on ventures as busy men are,
Bound to an inexorable result:
But like the birds or lilies
He seeks first the Kingdom, without care.
Nor need the free man remember
Any street or city, or keep campaigns
In his head, or countries for that matter
Or any other economy.

Under the blunt pine Elias becomes his own geography
(Supposing geography to be necessary at all),
Elias becomes his own wild bird, with God in the center,
His own pattern, surrounding the spirit
By which he is himself surrounded:

For the free man's road has neither beginning nor end.

(*Collected Poems*, pp. 244f)

The Trappist Abbey: Matins

When the full fields begin to smell of sunrise
And the valleys sing in their sleep,
The pilgrim moon pours over the solemn darkness
Her waterfalls of silence,
And then departs, up the long avenue of trees.

The stars hide, in the glade, their light, like tears
And tremble where some train runs, lost,
Baying in eastward mysteries of distance,
Where fire flares, somewhere, over a sink of cities.

Now kindle in the windows of this ladyhouse, my soul,
Your childish, clear awakeness:
Burn in the country night
Your wise and sleepless lamp,
For, from the frowning tower, the windy belfry,
Sudden the bells come, bridegrooms,
And fill the echoing dark with love and fear.

Wake in the windows of Gethsemani, my soul, my sister,
For the past years, with smokey torches, come,
Bringing betrayal from the burning world
And bloodying the glade with pitch flame.

Wake in the cloisters of the lonely night, my soul, my sister,
Where the apostles gather, who were, one time, scattered,
And mourn God's blood in the place of His betrayal,
And weep with Peter at the triple cock-crow.

(*Collected Poems*, pp. 45f)

The Communion

O sweet escape! O smiling flight!
O what bright secret breaks our jails of flesh?
For we are fled, among the shining vineyards,
And ride in praises in the hills of wheat,
To find our hero, in His tent of light!
O sweet escape, O smiling flight!

O sweet escape! O smiling flight!
The vineyards break our fetters with their laughter!
Our souls walk home as quiet as skies.
The snares that death, our subtle hunter, set,
Are all undone by beams of light!
O sweet escape! O smiling flight!

O sweet escape! O smiling flight!
Unlock our dark! And let us out of night!
And set us free to go to prison in this vineyard,
(Where, in the vines, the sweet and secret sun
Works our eternal rescue into wine)
O sweet Escape! O smiling flight!

We'll rob Your vines and raid Your hill of wheat,
Until you lock us, Jesus in Your jails of light!
O sweet escape! O smiling flight!

(*Collected Poems*, pp. 40f)

The Biography

Oh read the verses of the loaded scourges,
And what is written in their terrible remarks:
"The Blood runs down the walls of Cambridge town,
As useless as the waters of the narrow river —
While pub and alley gamble for His vesture."

Although my life is written on Christ's Body like a map,
The nails have printed in those open hands
More than the abstract names of sins,
More than the countries and the towns,
The names of streets, the numbers of houses,
The record of the days and nights,
When I have murdered Him in every square and street.

Lance and thorn, and scourge and nail
Have more than made His Flesh my chronicle
My journeys more than bite His bleeding feet.

Christ, from my cradle, I had known You everywhere,
And even though I sinned, I walked in You, and knew
        You were my world:
You were my France and England,
My seas and my America:
You were my life and air, and yet I would not own You.

Oh, when I loved You, even while I hated You,
Loving and yet refusing You in all the glories of Your universe

It was Your living Flesh I tore and trampled, not the air and
        earth:
Not that You feel us, in created things,
But knowing You, in them, made every sin a sacrilege;

And every act of greed became a desecration,
Spoiled and dishonored You as in Your Eucharist.

And yet with every wound You robbed me of a crime,
And as each blow was paid with Blood,
You paid me also each great sin with greater graces.
For even as I killed You,
You made Yourself a greater thief than any in Your company,
Stealing my sins into Your dying life,
Robbing me even of my death.

Where, on what cross my agony will come
I do not ask You:
For it is written and accomplished here,
On every Crucifix, on every altar,
It is my narrative that drowns and is forgotten
In Your five open Jordans,
Your voice that cries my: *"Consummatum est."*

If on Your Cross Your life and death and mine are one,
Love teaches me to read, in You, the rest of a new history.
I trace my days back to another childhood,
Exchanging as I go,
New York and Cuba for Your Galilee,
And Cambridge for Your Nazareth,
Until I come again to my beginning,
And find a manger, star and straw,
A pair of animals, some simple men,
And thus I learn that I was born,
Now not in France, but Bethlehem.

(*Collected Poems*, pp. 104f)

On the Anniversary of my Baptism

Certain waters are as blue as metal
Or as salt as sorrow.

Others wince like brass in the hammering sun,
Or stammer all over with tremors of shadow
That die as fast as the light winds
Whose flights surprise the promontories
And the marble bay.

Some are crowded everywhere, off-shore, with purple coral
Between the fleets of light that founder in the sand.
Others are full of yawls, or loud with launches,
Or sadder than the bitter smoke
Of tug and trawler, tramp and collier,

Or as grey as battle.
Oh! Since I was a baby in the Pyrenees,
When old St. Martin marked me for the cloister from
        high Canigou,
How many deeps, how many wicked seas
Went to befriend me with a flash of white-caps
Louder than laughter in the wind and sun,
Or sluggered all our brown bows gunwale-under
In their rowdy thunder —
Only to return me to the land.

Do you suppose that if the green Atlantic
Had ever cracked our brittle shell
And rifled all the cabins for their fruit of drunken passengers,
Do you suppose my sins,
Once we were sorted and disposed forever
Along the shelves of that profound, unvisited museum,

Would there have been immune,
Or learned to keep their coats of unreality
From the deep sea's most patient candying?

The day You made the waters,
And dragged them down from the dividing islands
And made them spring with fish,
You planned to bless the brine out of the seas
That were to be my death.

And this is the ninth November since my world's end and my
Genesis, When, with the sting of salt in my dry mouth,
Cross-crowned with water by the priest,
Stunned at the execution of my old companion, death,
And with the murder of my savage history,
You drowned me in the shallow font.

My eyes, swimming in unexpected infancy,
Were far too frail for such a favor:
They still close-kept the stone shell of their empty sepulchre:
But, though they saw none, guessed the new-come Trinity
That charged my sinews with His secret life.

(*Collected Poems*, pp. 155ff)

The Poet, to His Book

Now is the day of our farewell in fear, lean pages:
And shall I leave some blessing on the half of me you have
        devoured?
Were you, in clean obedience, my Cross,
Sent to exchange my life for Christ's in labor?
How shall the seeds upon those furrowed papers flower?

Or have I only bled to sow you full of stones and thorns,
Feeding my minutes to my own dead will?

Or will your little shadow fatten in my life's last hour
And darken for a space my gate to white eternity?
And will I wear you once again, in Purgatory,
Around my mad ribs like a shirt of flame?
Or bear you on my shoulders for a sorry jubilee
My Sinbad's burden?
Is that the way you'd make me both-ways' loser,
Paying the prayers and joys you stole of me,
You thirsty traitor, in my Trappist mornings!
Go, stubborn talker,
Find you a station on the loud world's corners,
And try there, (if your hands be clean) your length
        of patience:
Use there the rhythms that upset my silences,
And spend your pennyworth of prayer
There in the clamor of the Christless avenues:

And try to ransom some one prisoner
Out of those walls of traffic, out of the wheels of that
        unhappiness!

(*Collected Poems*, pp. 192f)

To the Immaculate Virgin, on a Winter Night

Lady, the night is falling and the dark
Steals all the blood from the scarred west.
The stars come out and freeze my heart
With drops of untouchable music, frail as ice
And bitter as the new year's cross.

Where in the world has any voice
Prayed to you, Lady, for the peace that's in your power?
In a day of blood and many beatings
I see the governments rise up, behind the steel horizon,
And take weapons and begin to kill.

Where in the world has any city trusted you?
Out where the soldiers camp the guns begin to thump
And another winter time comes down
To seal our years of ice.
The last train cries out
And runs in terror from this farmers' valley
Where all the little birds are dead.

The roads are white, the fields are mute
There are no voices in the wood
And trees make gallows up against the sharp-eyed stars.
Oh where will Christ be killed again
In the land of these dead men?

Lady, the night has got us by the heart
And the whole world is tumbling down.
And words turn to ice in my dry throat
Praying for a land without prayer.

Walking to you on water all winter
In a year that wants more war.

(*Collected Poems*, pp. 218f)

The Spiritual Master

Undoubtedly, Thomas Merton attracted greater notoriety as a social critic but he made his most profound and lasting contribution as a spiritual master.

Merton gave himself wholeheartedly to the spiritual quest. As St. Benedict, the author of the Rule he lived by, put it: he truly sought God. And he was ready to follow wherever that search led. Coupled with this, indeed intimately, his selflessness enabled him to share himself openly, almost nakedly. In addition he was a gifted writer with a frank and sincere style, indeed a passion to write, to put himself on paper. He was a good teacher, too. He enjoyed conveying knowledge in a clear and practical way.

Perhaps most important is that Merton was an existentialist. He was in touch with what is and he talked clearly and directly about what is. Merton certainly knew the Christian tradition. He had had relatively good biblical studies. He delved deeply into the Church Fathers. His exceptionally good knowledge of Latin allowed him to turn some of his favorite passages into fine English. After an introduction at Columbia, he studied the scholastics more thoroughly as he prepared for his ordination to the priesthood. He understood and appreciated the essentialist approach, yet he also understood that today's American found that approach largely unintelligible. In any case, he himself wrote in an existentialist mode. And that is one of the reasons why he has been the most effective Church writer of the twentieth century. He spoke of the deepest concerns of every thoughtful person and he spoke of them in a way that could be understood easily.

Merton's writing on the human person and that person's quest of ultimate meaning are extensive. For the most part they do not take the form of a book. His early attempt to write a complete synthesis of the spiritual journey led to his only experience of writer's block. When he did finally complete the book, *Ascent to Truth*, it was not one of his better works. Only in the last days of his life did he again attempt to write a complete book on prayer. But even this, *The Climate of Monastic Prayer*, which he sent to the publisher on the eve of his departure from Gethsemani, was more like an expansion of an earlier essay. Another book he was working on at that time, *The Inward Journey*, he declared incomplete. The rest of his books, those that are not edited journals, are in fact collections of essays or poems. But these essays explore every facet of the human journey and collected in volumes they present a comprehensive exploration of the chosen matter.

Merton, in the end understood well the human person and transcendent human dignity. And through faith and experience he knew to what the human person is called. The way thereto he explored generously and fearlessly. Indeed, that exploration took him on his last fateful journey as he eagerly sought the light that other cultures and religious traditions had to cast on what he had already discovered in his own — and in others by correspondence and reading.

We offer here a broad sampling of Merton's writings on the inward journey of the human adventure. Inevitably they will invite the reader to seek out his fully developed ideas in the complete works.

I Merely Need to Be Myself

We are warmed by fire, not by the smoke of the fire. We are carried over the sea by a ship, not by the wake of a ship. So too, what we are is to be sought in the invisible depths of our own being, not in our outward reflection in our own acts. We must find our real selves not in the froth stirred up by the impact of our being upon the beings around us, but in our own soul which is the principle of all our acts.

But my soul is hidden and invisible. I cannot see it directly, for it is hidden even from myself. Nor can I see my own eyes. They are too close to me for me to see them. They are not meant to see themselves. I know I have eyes when I see other things with them.

I can see my eyes in a mirror. My soul can also reflect itself in the mirror of its own activity. But what is seen in the mirror is only the reflection of who I am, not my true being. The mirror of words and actions only partly manifest my being.

The words and acts that proceed from myself and are accomplished outside myself are dead things compared with the hidden life from which they spring. These acts are transient and superficial. They are quickly gone, even though their effects may persist for a little while. But the soul itself remains. Much depends on how the soul sees itself in the mirror of its own activity.

My soul does not find itself unless it acts. Therefore it must act. Stagnation and inactivity bring spiritual death. But my soul must not project itself entirely into the outward effects of its activity. I do not need to *see* myself, I merely need to *be* myself. I must think and act like a living being, but I must not plunge my whole self into what I think and do, or seek always to find myself in the work I have done. The soul that projects itself entirely into activity, and seeks itself outside itself in the work of its own will is like a madman who sleeps on the sidewalk in front of his house instead of living inside where it is quiet and warm. The soul that throws itself outdoors in order to find itself in the effects of its own work is like a fire that has no desire to burn but seeks only to go up in smoke.

The reason why men are so anxious to see themselves, instead of being content to be themselves, is that they do not really believe in their own existence. And they do not fully believe that they exist because they do not believe in God. This is equally true of those who say they believe in God (without actually putting their faith into practice) and of those who do not even pretend to have any faith.

In either case, the loss of faith has evolved at the same time as complete loss of all sense of reality. Being means nothing to those who hate and fear what they themselves are. Therefore they cannot have peace in their own reality (which reflects the reality of God). They must struggle to escape their true being, and verify a false existence by constantly viewing what they themselves do. They have to keep looking in the mirror for reassurance. What do they expect to see? Not themselves! They are hoping for some sign that they have become the god they hope to become by means of their own frantic activity — invulnerable, all powerful, infinitely wise, unbearably beautiful, unable to die!

When a man constantly looks and looks at himself in the mirror of his own acts, his spiritual double vision splits him into two people. And if he strains his eyes hard enough, he forgets which one is real. In fact, reality is no longer found either in himself or in his shadow. The substance has gone out of itself into the shadow, and he has become two shadows instead of one real person.

Then the battle begins. Whereas one shadow was meant to praise the other, now one shadow accuses the other. The activity that was meant to exalt him, reproaches and condemns him. It is never real enough. Never active enough. The less he is able to *be* the more he has to *do*. He becomes his own slave driver — a shadow whipping a shadow to death, because it cannot produce reality, infinitely substantial reality, out of his own nonentity.

Then comes fear. The shadow becomes afraid of the shadow. He who "is not" becomes terrified at the things he cannot do. Whereas for a while he had illusions of infinite power, miraculous sanctity (which he was able to guess at in the mirror of his virtuous actions), now it has all changed. Tidal waves of nonentity, of powerlessness, of hopelessness surge up within him at every action he attempts.

Then the shadow judges and hates the shadow who is not a god, and who can do absolutely nothing.

Self-contemplation leads to the most terrible despair: the despair of a god that hates himself to death. This is the ultimate perversion of man who was made in the image and likeness of the true God, who was made to love eternally and perfectly an infinite good — a good (note this well) which he was to find *dwelling within himself!*

In order to find God in ourselves, we must stop looking at ourselves, stop checking and verifying ourselves in the mirror of our own futility, and be content to *be* in him and to do whatever he wills, according to our limitations, judging our acts not in the light of our own illusions, but in the light of his reality which is all around us in the things and people we live with. All men seek peace first of all with themselves. That is necessary, because we do not naturally find rest even in our own being. We have to learn to commune with ourselves before we can communicate with other men and with God. A man who is not at peace with himself necessarily projects his interior fighting into the society of those he lives with, and spreads a contagion of conflict all around him. Even when he tries to do good to others his efforts are hopeless, since he does not know how to do good to himself. In moments of wildest idealism he may take it into his head to make other people happy: and in doing so he will overwhelm them with his own unhappiness. He seeks to find himself somehow in the work of making others happy. Therefore he throws himself into the work. As a result he gets out of the work all that he put into it: his own confusion, his own disintegration, his own unhappiness.

It is useless to try to make peace with ourselves by being pleased with everything we have done. In order to settle down in the quiet of our own being we must learn to be detached from the results of our own activity. We must withdraw ourselves, to some extent, from effects that are beyond our control and be content with the good will and the work that are the quiet expressions of our inner life. We must be content to live without watching ourselves live, to work without expecting an immediate reward, to love without an instantaneous satisfaction, and to exist without any special recognition.

It is only when we are detached from ourselves that we can be at peace with ourselves. We cannot find happiness in our work if we are always extending ourselves beyond ourselves and beyond the sphere of our work in order to find ourselves greater than we are.

Our Christian destiny is, in fact, a great one: but we cannot achieve greatness unless we lose all interest in being great. For our own idea of greatness is illusory, and if we pay too much attention to it we will be lured out of the peace and stability of the being God gave us, and seek to live in a myth we have created for ourselves. It is, therefore, a very great thing to be little, which is to say: to be ourselves. And when we are truly ourselves we lose most of the futile self-consciousness that keeps us constantly comparing ourselves with others in order to see how big we are.

(*No Man Is an Island*, pp. 117–122)

The Present is Our Right Place

First of all, we must be present to ourselves.

The cares and preoccupations of life draw us away from ourselves. As long as we give ourselves to these things, our minds are not at home. They are drawn out of their own reality into the illusion to which they tend. They let go of the actuality which they have and which they are, in order to follow a flock of possibilities. But possibilities have wings, and our minds must take flight from themselves in order to follow them into the sky. If we live with possibilities we are exiles from the present which is given us by God to be our own, homeless and displaced in a future or a past which are not ours because they are always beyond our reach. The present is our right place and we can lay hands on whatever it offers us. Recollection is the only thing that can give us the power to do so. But before we explain that, let us return to the idea that recollection makes us present to ourselves.

As long as we are in this life, we both are and are not. We are constantly changing, and yet the person who changes is always the same person. Even his changes express his personality, and develop it, and confirm him for what he is.

A man is a free being who is always changing into himself. This changing is never merely indifferent. We are always getting either better or worse. Our development is measured by our acts of free choice, and we make ourselves according to the pattern of our desires.

If our desires reach out for the things that we were created to have and to make and to become, then we will develop into what we were truly meant to be.

But if our desires reach out for things that have no meaning for the growth of our spirit, if they lose themselves in dreams or passions or illusions, we will be false to ourselves and in the end our lives will proclaim that we have lied to ourselves and to other men and to God. We will judge ourselves as aliens and exiles from ourselves and from God.

In hell, there is no recollection. The damned are exiled not only from God and from other men, but even from themselves.

(*No Man Is an Island*, pp. 219–220)

Absences of God

God, who is everywhere, never leaves us. Yet he seems sometimes to be present, sometimes absent. If we do not know him well, we do not realize that he may be more present to us when he is absent than when he is present.

There are two absences of God. One is an absence that condemns us, the other an absence that sanctifies us.

In the absence that is condemnation, God "knows us not" because we have put some other god in his place, and refuse to be known by him. In the absence that sanctifies, God empties the soul of every image that might become an idol and of every concern that might stand between our face and his Face.

In the first absence, he is present, but his presence is denied by the presence of an idol. God is present to the enemy we have placed between ourselves and him in mortal sin.

In the second absence he is present, and his presence is affirmed and adored by the absence of everything else. He is closer to us than we are to ourselves, although we do not see him.

Whoever seeks to catch him and hold him loses him. He is like the wind that blows where it pleases. You who love him must love him as arriving from where you do not know and as going where you do not know. Your spirit must seek to be as clean and as free as his own Spirit, in order to follow him wherever he goes. Who are we to call ourselves either clean or free, unless he makes us so?

If he should teach us how to follow him into the wilderness of his own freedom, we will no longer know where we are, because we are with him who is everywhere and nowhere at the same time.

Those who love only his apparent presence cannot follow the Lord wherever he goes. They do not love him perfectly if they do not allow him to be absent.

(*No Man Is an Island*, pp. 237–238)

In the Silence

God our Creator and Savior has given us a language in which he can be talked about, since faith cometh by hearing and our tongues are the keys that open heaven to others.

But when the Lord comes as a Bridegroom there remains nothing to be said except that he is coming, and that we must go out to meet him. *Ecce Sponsus venit! Exite obviam ei!* ["Behold the Bridegroom cometh, go you forth to meet him."]

After that we go forth to find him in solitude. There we communicate with him alone, without words, without discursive thoughts, in the silence of our whole being.

When what we say is meant for no one else but him, it can hardly be said in language. What is not meant to be related is not even experienced on a level that can be clearly analyzed. We know that it must not be told, because it cannot.

But before we come to that which is unspeakable and unthinkable, the spirit hovers on the frontiers of language, wondering whether or not to stay on its own side of the border, in order to have something to bring back to other men. This is the test of those who wish to cross the frontier. If they are not ready to leave their own ideas and their own words behind them, they cannot travel further.

Do not desire chiefly to be cherished and consoled by God; desire above all to love him. . . .

There must be a time of day when the man who makes plans forgets his plans, and acts as if he had no plans at all.

There must be a time of day when the man who has to speak falls very silent. And his mind forms no more propositions, and he asks himself: Did they have a meaning?

There must be a time when the man of prayer goes to pray as if it were the first time in his life he had ever prayed; when the man of resolutions puts his resolutions aside as if they had all been broken, and he learns a different wisdom: distinguishing the sun from the moon, the stars from the darkness, the sea from the dry land, and the night sky from the shoulder of a hill.

(*No Man Is an Island*, pp. 254–260)

When He Has Found His Vocation

A man knows when he has found his vocation when he stops thinking about how to live and begins to live. Thus, if one is called to be a solitary, he will stop wondering how he is to live and start living peacefully only when he is in solitude. But if one is not called to a solitary life, the more he is alone the more will he worry about living and forget to live. When we are not living up to our true vocation, thought deadens our life, or substitutes itself for life, or gives in to life so that our life drowns out our thinking and stifles the voice of conscience. When we find our vocation — thought and life are one.

Suppose one has found completeness in his true vocation. Now everything is in unity, in order, at peace. Now work no longer interferes with prayer or prayer with work. Now contemplation no longer needs to be a special "state" that removes one from the ordinary things going on around him for God penetrates all. One does not have to think of giving an account of oneself to anyone but him.

(*Thoughts in Solitude*, 87)

To Live in Him

It is a greater thing and a better prayer to live in him who is infinite, and to rejoice that he is infinite, than to strive always to press his infinity into the narrow space of our own hearts. As long as I am content to know that he is infinitely greater than I, and that I cannot know him unless he shows himself to me, I will have peace and he will be near me and in me, and I will rest in him. But as soon as I desire to know and enjoy him for myself, I reach out to do violence to him who evades me and in so doing I do violence to myself and fall back upon myself in sorrow and anxiety, knowing that he has gone his way.

In true prayer, although every silent moment remains the same, every moment is a new discovery of a new silence, a new penetration into that eternity in which all things are always new. We know, by fresh discovery, the deep reality that is our concrete here and now and in the depths of that reality we receive from the Father of light, truth, wisdom and peace. These are the reflections of God in our souls which are made to his image and likeness.

(*Thoughts in Solitude*, pp. 97–98)

God's Immanence

Grace does not take hold of us as if we were planes or rockets guided by remote control. Yet there is a rather common tendency among spiritual men to imagine themselves as hollow, empty beings entirely governed and moved by a remote supernatural agency from outside and above themselves. This indeed pays homage to the idea that God is infinitely above man. But it entirely ignores the equally important truth of God's immanence within man. The spiritual man is not and cannot be a mere puppet, agitated from above by invisible wires which he himself does not perceive. If that were so, the spiritual life would be the worst kind of self-alienation. Sanctity would be nothing but schizophrenia.

In order to see the absurdity of such thoughts, we need only go back to St. Paul and read such words as these: "The charity of God is poured forth in our hearts by the Holy Spirit who has been given to us." [Romans 5:5] Not only is divine love in us, as the intimate principle of the highest kind of life, awareness, and activity, but the Spirit of God himself dwells in us as the Gift of God, and he is there to be known and loved. He ever desires his presence to be recognized in contemplative prayer. "But you shall know him (the Spirit), because he will dwell with you, and be in you." [John 14:17] . . .

The union of the Christian with God is the exact opposite of a Promethean exploit, because the Christian is not trying to steal something from God that God does not want him to have. On the contrary, he is striving with his whole heart to fulfill the will of God and lay hands upon that which God created him to receive. And what is that? It is nothing else but a participation in the life, and wisdom, and joy and peace of God himself. This is greater than any other gift, higher than any other power. It is supreme freedom, the most perfect fulfillment. It has been called by the Fathers of the Church the *divinization* (*theosis*) of man. It is the ultimate in man's self-realization, for when it is perfected, man not only discovers his true self, but finds himself to be mystically one with the God by whom he has been elevated and transformed.

The war between life and death within us is a war in which we are fighting not only for our life and our freedom, but also, at the same time, for the glory and kingdom of God. For when the truth of Christ has made us free, then we are what we are meant to be: images of the Divine Father, sons who work with the Father to establish his Kingdom of freedom

(*The New Man*, pp. 45–48)

First Find Ourselves

To resume all these ideas, the image of God is the summit of spiritual consciousness in man. It is his highest peak of self-realization. This is achieved not merely by reflection of his actual, present self: one's actual self may be far from "real," since it may be profoundly alienated from one's own deep spiritual identity. To reach one's "real self" one must, in fact, be delivered by grace, virtue and asceticism, from that illusory and false "self" whom we have created by our habits of selfishness and by our constant flights from reality. In order to find God, whom we can only find in and through the depths of our own soul, we must therefore first find ourselves. To use common figures of speech, we must "return to ourselves," we must "come to our selves." Our ordinary life, cluttered and obstructed as it is by our own bad habits of thought and action as well as by the bad habits of the society we live in, is little more than a semi-conscious, torpid kind of existence when it is compared with the real life of our deep selves — the life that we are all supposed to be leading. To awaken to the realities of the spirit and to discover the image of God within us is therefore something quite different from a Platonic awakening to the spirituality of our formal human essence as distinguished from the concrete materiality that weighs us down. The Christian view does not make an abstract division between matter and spirit. It plunges into existential depths of the concrete union of body and soul which makes up the human person, and by clearing the spiritual temple of all those ways of thinking which obstruct our inward vision, opens the way to an existential communion at the same time with ourselves and with God in the actual, subsisting, spiritual reality of our own inviolable being. In this way, the body is not discarded (which is in any case not possible) but elevated and spiritualized. Man is not cut in half, he is drawn together and finds himself more of one piece, more integrated than ever before.

(*The New Man*, pp. 63–64)

We Become Real

The first step in all this is to recognize our true condition. Before we can ever hope to find ourselves in God, we must clearly recognize the fact that we are far from him. Before we can realize who we really are, we must become conscious of the fact that the person we think we are, here and now, is at best an imposter and a stranger. We must constantly question his motives and penetrate his disguises, otherwise our attempts at self knowledge are bound to fail, for if we fully and complacently acquiesce in our own illusion of who we are, our "self-knowledge" will only strive to reinforce our identification of ourselves with this imposter.

Nevertheless, even the natural man is able, if he is honest, to make a beginning in the work of self-knowledge. Socrates used to go around Athens confounding the "right-thinking" citizens, the magistrates who assumed they knew the secret of words and of this power. In the end they killed him because he told them, too clearly, that they did not dare to face such questions. The judicial murder was committed in the name of the gods. But that was precisely the most eloquent admission of the fact that these people feared to face their own unreality, which they defended in the projected "reality" of gods in whom they could not really believe.

It is a spiritual disaster for a man to rest content with his exterior identity, with his passport picture of himself. Is his life merely in his fingerprints? Does he really exist because his name has been inscribed in *Who's Who*? Is his picture in the Sunday paper any safe indication that he is not a zombie? If that is who he thinks he is, then he is already done for, because he is no longer alive, even though he may seem to exist. Actually he is only pushing the responsibility for his existence onto society. Instead of facing the question of who he is, he assumes he is a person because there appear to be other persons who recognize him when he walks down the street.

Since we are made in the image and likeness of God, there is no other way for us to find out who we are than by finding in ourselves the divine image. Now this image, which is present in every one of us by nature, can indeed be known by rational inference. But that is not enough to give us a real experience of our own identity. It is hardly better than inferring that we exist because other people act as if we existed.

Just as some men have to struggle to recover a natural, spontaneous realization of their own capacity for life and movement and physical enjoyment, so all men have to struggle to regain the spontaneous and vital awareness of their *spirituality*, of the fact that they have a soul that is capable of coming to life and experiencing profound and hidden values which the flesh and its senses can never discover alone. And this spirituality in man is identified with the divine image in our soul.

St. Thomas gives us a concrete and thoroughly existential intuition of the divine image when he says that it is not only a static "representation" of something in the divine essence, but a *dynamic tendency* that carries us toward union with God. It is a kind of gravitational sensitivity to the things of God. "The image of God is seen in the soul insofar as the soul is carried, or is able to be carried, towards God."

Now if we are to recognize the image in ourselves, it is not sufficient for us to enter into ourselves. It is not enough for us to realize that the spirituality of our nature makes us potentially god-like. The potentiality must be actualized. How? By knowledge and love: or, more precisely, by a knowledge of God that is inseparable from an experience of love. As St. Thomas says, in the context of the words quoted above: "The image of God is in the soul according to the knowledge it conceives of God and according to the love that flows from that knowledge."

Self-realization in this true religious sense is then less an awareness of ourselves than an awareness of the God to whom we are drawn in the depths of our own being. We become real, and experience our actuality, not when we pause to reflect upon our own self as an isolated individual entity, but rather when, transcending ourselves and passing beyond reflection, we center our whole soul upon the God who is our life. That is to say we fully "realize" ourselves when we cease to be conscious of ourselves in separateness and know nothing but the one God who is above all knowledge.

We fully realize ourselves when all our awareness is of another — of him who is utterly "Other" than all being because he is infinitely above them. The image of God is brought to life in us when it breaks free from the shroud and the tomb in which our self-consciousness had kept it prisoner, and loses itself in a total consciousness of him who is holy. This is one of the main ways in which "he that would save his life will lose it." [Luke 9:24]. . .

God will not reduce the distance between ourselves and him by any compromise with our own weakness and imperfection. With him there is and there can be no compromise. The mercy, which is a total giving of his love to us, is anything but compromise, since it demands, in return, the total gift of ourselves to him, and this gift of ourselves is obstructed, within ourselves, by our own self-alienation.

When the light of God's truth begins to find its way through the mists of illusion and self-deception with which we have unconsciously surrounded ourselves, and when the image of God within us begins to return to itself, the false self which we inherited from Adam begins to experience the strange panic that Adam felt when, after his sin, he hid in the trees of the garden because he heard the voice of the Lord God in the afternoon.

If we are to recover our own identity, and return to God by the way Adam came in his fall, we must learn to stop saying: "I heard you in the garden, and I was afraid, because I was naked. And I hid." [Genesis 2:10] We must cast away the "aprons of leaves" and the "garments of skins" which the Fathers of the Church variously interpret as passions, and attachments to earthly things, and fixation in our own rigid determination to be someone other than our true selves.

(*The New Man*, pp. 119–128)

The Free Spiritual Option

Freedom of choice is not, of itself, the perfection of liberty.
But it helps us take our first step toward freedom or slavery,
spontaneity or compulsion. The free man is the one whose
choices have given him the power to stand on his own feet and
determine his own life according to the higher light and spirit
that are in him. The slave, in the spiritual order, is the man
whose choices have destroyed all spontaneity in him and have
delivered him over, bound hand and foot, to his own compul-
sions, idiosyncrasies and illusion, so that he never does what
he really wants to do, but only what he has to do. His spirit is
not in command, and therefore he cannot run his own life. He
is commanded by his own weak flesh and its passions — fear,
greed, lust, insecurity, untruthfulness, envy, cruelty, servility,
and all the rest.

He who is a slave is therefore never stable, never secure. He
is always at the mercy of change. Therefore he cannot rest. He
cannot defend himself against himself until he begins to
make spiritual choices: and he cannot make any of these until
he learns to resist the blinding compulsion of passion. In other
words he cannot live like a man, by reason, until he trains
himself not to live like an animal, by instinct. For since we are
not meant to live by instincts, like the animals, our instinctive
life is insufficient to sustain us at the proper level of our spiritual being, although it may be all right in itself.

If we are to live as free men in the supernatural order, we
must make free supernatural choices. We do this by obeying
God out of love. The discourse at the Last Supper is full of
remarks about the importance of this obedience: but we will
never understand the obedience preached by Christ unless we
remember, always, that his obedience is not merely justice, it
is love. It is not merely the homage of our wills to God's
authority, it is the free union of our wills with God's love. We

do not obey God because we have to but because we want to. That is precisely the nature of the free spiritual option that makes us sons of God. The Fathers of the Church, who contemplated the mystery of this freedom of the spirit, were perfectly aware that servility was incompatible with our divine sonship. We cannot become sons of God by an obedience that is merely a blind renunciation of our own autonomy. On the contrary, spiritual freedom consecrates our autonomy to Christ and, in Christ, to the Father, so that we may love the Father with his own spirit of freedom, or, so to speak, with his own autonomy. Where this truth is not grasped, Christianity dies and gives place to the legalism which nailed Christ to the Cross.

(*The New Man*, pp. 178–180)

The Most Perfect Possible Unity

To know the one God as the Creator of the universe is one thing. To know the Father as sending the Son and revealing himself in the Son is quite another. The first knowledge is a knowledge "about" God, the second is a penetration into the infinite mystery of God himself. We may truly apprehend something about God's love when we know him as the source of our own being. But we learn, and learn by experience that God is love — *Deus caritas est* — when we find that we ourselves have become identified with the Son whom the Father has sent, and that the Father sends the Son from within ourselves, and that the Holy Spirit teaches us the identity of the Father and the Son. This Divine Spirit leading us to oneness with the Word, enlightens us as to the infinite love which comes forth eternally from the Father as from a Beginning that has no beginning.

Now we begin to see the full meaning of Jesus's words: "I live, and you shall live." What is this life? It is eternal life, mystical life in the knowledge of "thee, the one true God, and Jesus Christ whom thou hast sent." Much more, it is the knowledge promised by Christ to the Apostles "in that day" when they should receive his Spirit. "In that day you will know that I am in my Father and you in me and I in you."

This last verse from St. John is a most complete expression of the New Adam. The Mystical Body of Christ is the Body of those who are united with one another and with the Father and the Son by a union of charity so close that it is analogous to the circumincession in which the Father dwells in the Son and the Son in the Father. Indeed, our status as sons of God depends on the fact that our unity with Christ makes us dwell in the Father as does the Son. These theological expressions strive to express the most perfect possible unity. The man, therefore, who, enlightened by the Spirit of God, discovers in himself this union with the Father in the Son and with all men in Christ, is at the same time unified in the highest possible degree within himself and perfectly united with all who are one with Christ.

The force that holds this unity together is charity, and that is why everything that Christ tells us about union with God and the knowledge of the Father is centered upon charity. His own union with the Father depends on the love of the Father for him. Our union with him depends on his love for us, which is simply the extension of the Father's love, through him, to ourselves. And the charity of Christ, which springs from the Father as from its hidden and infinite source, goes out through us to those who have not yet known him, and unites them, through Christ in us, to the Father. By our love for other men, we enable them to discover Christ in themselves and to pass through Christ to the Source, the Beginning of all life, the Father, present and hidden in the depths of their own being.

Finding him, they who have long been torn and divided by the disintegrating force of their own illusions are able to discover and integrate themselves in one.

(*The New Man*, pp. 188–190)

To Be without Anxiety in the Midst of Anxiety

In our age everything has to be a "problem." Ours is a time of anxiety because we have willed it to be so. Our anxiety is not imposed on us by force from outside. We impose it on our world and upon one another from within ourselves.

Sanctity in such an age means, no doubt, traveling from the area of anxiety or perhaps it may mean learning, from God, to be without anxiety in the midst of anxiety.

Fundamentally, as Max Picard points out, it probably comes to this: living in a silence which so reconciles the contradictions within us that, although they remain within us, they cease to be a problem.

Contradictions have always existed in the soul of man. But it is only when we prefer analysis to silence that they become a constant and insoluble problem. We are not meant to resolve all contradictions but to live with them and rise above them and see them in the light of exterior and objective values which make them trivial by comparison.

Silence, then, belongs to the substance of sanctity. In silence and hope are formed the strength of the Saints.

When solitude was a problem, I had no solitude. When it ceased to be a problem I found I already possessed it, and could have possessed it all along. Yet still it was a problem because I knew after all that a merely subjective and inward solitude, the fruit of an effort at interiorization, would never be enough. Solitude has to be objective and concrete. It has to be a communion in something greater than the world, as great as Being itself, in order that in its deep peace we may find God.

(Thoughts in Solitude, pp. 82–83)

It's a Risky Thing to Pray

It's a risky thing to pray, and the danger is that our very prayers get between God and us. The great thing in prayer is not to pray, but to go directly to God. If saying your prayers is an obstacle to prayer, cut it out. Let Jesus pray. Thank God Jesus is praying. Forget yourself. Enter into the prayer of Jesus. Let him pray in you.... The best way to pray is: stop. Let prayer pray within you, whether you know it or not. This means a deep awareness of our true inner identity.... But the point is that we need not justify ourselves. By grace we are Christ. Our relationship with God is that of Christ to the Father in the Holy Spirit.

(Thomas Merton, Monk, pp. 89–90)

Our True Personality

After all, what is your personal identity? It is what you really are, your real self. None of us is what he thinks he is, or what other people think he is, still less what his passport says he is. Many of us think, no doubt, that we are what we would like to be. And it is fortunate for most of us that we are mistaken. We do not generally know what is good for us. That is because, in Bernard's language, our true personality has been concealed under the disguise of a false self, the *ego* whom we tend to worship in place of God. The monastic ascesis is entirely directed against this *ego*. To the worldling, who knows no other "self" than this shadow of himself, the Cistercian life will evidently spell the destruction of everything he is accustomed to think of as his real personality. But the monk who has given himself, without return, to God and to the formation prescribed by the Rule soon discovers that monastic obedience and penance are rapidly delivering him from the one force that has prevented him all his life from knowing his true self.

We are what we love. If we love God, in whose image we were created, we discover ourselves in him and we cannot help being happy: we have already achieved something of the fullness of being for which we were destined in our creation. If we love everything else but God, we contradict the image born in our very essence, and we cannot help being unhappy, because we are living a caricature of what we are meant to be.

(*The Waters of Siloe*, pp. 349–350)

The Spiritual Life
is Not an Exclusively Private Affair

Contrary to what has been taught in recent centuries in the West, the spiritual or interior life is not an exclusively private affair. (In reality, the deepest and most authentic Western traditions are at one with those of the East on this point.) The spiritual life of one person is simply the life of all manifesting itself in him. While it is very necessary to emphasize the truth that as the person deepens his own thought in silence he enters into a deeper understanding of and communion with the spirit of his entire people (or of his Church), it is also important to remember that as he becomes engaged in the crucial struggles of his people, in seeking justice and truth together with his brothers, he tends to liberate the truth in himself by seeking true liberty for all. Thus Plato taught that "to philosophize and concern oneself with politics is one and the same thing, and to wrestle with the sophist means at the same time to defend the city against tyranny."

So true was this that Socrates would not turn his back on the equivocation of his fellow citizens and their betrayal of truth, even when their hatred of reason meant his own death.

The "spiritual space" created by the Polis was still, in any event, the only place for the philosopher. True, in an imperfect city a fully human life was not possible, and hence *a fortiori* the perfect philosophical life was out of the question. "The philosopher has no place in the city except at its helm." Yet if he is not only silenced but even condemned unjustly to death, it remains his function as philosopher to teach the city truth by his death rather than fly into exile or withdraw into private life, since a purely private existence could not be fully "philosophical."

(*Gandhi on Non-Violence*, pp. 6–7)

It is Natural to Have Mature Friendships

If I regard friendship as a distraction, then probably it is. And if it's a distraction, that means my friend is an object. If the friend is a distraction, the friend is a foreign object in my mind. The answer is not to get rid of friends and to get rid of foreign objects, but to love people in such a way that they're *not* a foreign object. If you get a foreign object in your eye, it hurts. But if you just get light in your eye, it doesn't hurt at all. We always go back to the central thing. Somebody you love is not a foreign object because you are not foreign to yourself and the person you love is your other self. But we just don't arrive at this by decree. If, in fact, I do love someone else as a foreign object, as a source of satisfaction, I can't say I don't. Usually we talk about a disinterested love, and this is very good. But maybe our love is sentimental and dependent on the other person. When you love someone as an object, what's the consequence? That person has to remain an object in order for you to get the satisfaction you want. You exploit the person. To keep someone as an object is to keep that person in a subservient position, something to be used for your own pleasure. This is sentimental friendship. The real harm lies in "babying" someone, treating an adult as a minor.

When it comes to spiritual virginity, there is such a thing as friendship with other people which is a gift of God. It's not something that can be arrived at just by being smart. It is natural to have mature friendships in which you love the other person because he or she is your other self. It's not distracting at all. You see things in more or less the same way and there's mutual support. A relationship like this can become deeply spiritual because you are, practically speaking, the same person. Therefore, you don't need to rely on it, to be dependent; it doesn't have to be there all the time. I think we've gotten a little more sophisticated on these points, don't you?

(*The Springs of Contemplation*, pp. 116–118)

What a Spiritual Life Really Is

Nourished by the Sacraments and formed by the prayer and teaching of the Church, we need seek nothing but the particular place willed for us by God within the Church. When we find that place, our life and our prayer both at once become extremely simple.

Then we discover what the spiritual life really is. It is not a matter of doing one good work rather than another, of living in one place rather than in another, of praying in one way rather than in another.

It is not a matter of any special psychological effect in our own soul. It is the silence of our whole being in compunction and adoration before God, in the habitual realization that he is everything and we are nothing, that he is the Center to which all things tend, and to whom all our actions must be directed. That our life and strength proceed from him, that both in life and in death we depend entirely on him, that the whole course of our life is foreknown by him and falls into the plan of his wise and merciful Providence, that it is absurd to live as though without him, for ourselves, by ourselves; that all our plans and spiritual ambitions are useless unless they come from him and end in him and that, in the end, the only thing that matters is his glory.

(*Thoughts in Solitude*, pp. 52–53)

We Ruin Our Life of Prayer

We ruin our life of prayer if we are constantly examining our prayer and seeking the fruit of prayer in a peace that is nothing more than a psychological process. The only thing to seek in contemplative prayer is God; and we seek him successfully when we realize that we cannot find him unless he shows himself to us, and yet at the same time that he would not have inspired us to seek him unless we had already found him.

(*Thoughts in Solitude*, p. 53)

There Are Many Levels of Attention in Prayer

There are many levels of attention at prayer.

First of all, there is purely exterior attention. We "say prayers" with out lips, but our hearts are not following what we say although we think we would like to mean what we are saying. If we do not cultivate something better than this, we will seldom really pray. If we are quite content to pray without paying attention to our prayer or to God, it shows we have not much idea of who God is, and that we do not really appreciate the grace and the privilege of being able to speak to him in prayer. For prayer is a gift of God, a gift which is by no means given to all men. Perhaps it is given to few because so few desire it, and of those who have received it few have received it with gratitude.

At other times, we think of God in prayer but our thoughts of him are not concerned with prayer. They are thoughts about him that do not establish any contact with him. So, while we pray, we are speculating about God and about the spiritual life, or composing sermons, or drawing up theological arguments. These thoughts are all right in their place, but if we take prayer seriously we will not call them prayer. For such thoughts cannot satisfy the soul that desires to find God in prayer. On the contrary, they leave it with a feeling of emptiness and dissatisfaction. At the same time, when one is really a man of prayer, speculative thoughts about God in the time of study or of intellectual work can often lead into prayer and give place to it; but only on condition that prayer is more to him than speculation.

Again, in prayer we are distracted by our spiritual difficulties, the problems of our state in life, the duties we have to face. It is not possible to avoid such distractions all the time, but if we know what prayer means and know who God is, we will be able to turn these thoughts themselves into motives of prayer. But we will not be satisfied with such prayer as this. It is good, indeed, to turn distractions into material for petition, but it is better not to be distracted, or at least not to be drawn away from God by our distractions.

Then there is the prayer that is well used: words or thoughts serve their purpose and lead our minds and hearts to God, and in our prayer we receive light to apply these thoughts to our own problems and difficulties, to those of our friends, or to those of the Church. But sometimes this prayer, which is, of course, valid, leaves our hearts unsatisfied because it is more concerned with our problems, with our friends, and ourselves, than it is with God. However, if we are humble men, we will be grateful for ever so little light in our prayer, and will not complain too much, for it is a great thing to receive even a little light from so great a God.

There is a better way of prayer, a greater gift from God, in which we pass through our prayer to him, and love him. We taste the goodness of his infinite mercy. We know that we are indeed his sons, although we know our unworthiness to be called the sons of God. We know his infinite mercy in Jesus, and we know the meaning of the fact that we, who are sinners, indeed have a Savior. And we learn what it is to know the Father in this Savior, Jesus, his Son. We enter thus into a great mystery which cannot be explained, but only experienced. But in this prayer we still remain conscious of ourselves, we can reflect upon ourselves, and realize that we are the subjects of this great experience of love, as well as the objects of God's love.

In the beginning this reflexive quality in our prayer does not disturb us. But as we mature in the spiritual life it begins to be a source of unrest and dissatisfaction. We are ashamed to be so much aware of ourselves in our prayer. We wish we were not in the way. We wish our love for God were no longer spoiled and clouded by any return upon ourselves. We wish we were no longer aware that we rejoiced in his love, for we fear that our rejoicing might end in selfishness and self-complacency. And although we are grateful for the consolation and the light of his love, we wish we ourselves could disappear and see only Jesus. These two moments of prayer are like the two phases of the Apostles' vision of the Transfigured Christ on Mount Tabor. At first Peter, James and John were delighted with the vision of Jesus, Moses and Elias. They thought it would be a fine thing to build three tabernacles and stay there on the mountain forever. But they were overshadowed by a cloud, and a voice came out of the cloud striking them with fear, and when they regained their vision they saw no one but Jesus alone.

So too there is another stage in our prayer, when consolation gives place to fear. It is a place of darkness and anguish and of conversion: for here a great change takes place in our spirit. All our love for God appears to us to have been full of imperfections, as indeed it has. We begin to doubt that we have ever loved him. With shame and sorrow we find that our love was full of complacency, and that although we thought ourselves modest, we overflowed with conceit. We were too sure of ourselves, not afraid of illusion, not afraid to be recognized by other men as men of prayer. Now we see things in a different light, for we are in the cloud, and the voice of the Father fills our hearts with unrest and fear, telling us that we must no longer see ourselves: and yet, to our terror, Jesus does not appear to us and all that we see is — ourselves. Then what we find in our souls becomes terrible to us. Instead of complacently calling ourselves sinners (and secretly believing ourselves just) we begin to find that the sins of our past life were really sins, and really *our* sins — and we have not regretted them! And that since the time when we were grave sinners, we have still sinned without realizing it, because we were too sure we were the friends of God, and we have taken his graces lightly, or taken them to ourselves, and turned them to our own selfish profit, and used them for our own vanity, and even exploited them to lift ourselves above other men, so that in many ways we have turned the love of God into selfishness and have reveled in his gifts without thanking him or using them for his glory.

Then we begin to see that it is just and right that we be abandoned by God, and left to face many and great temptations. Nor do we complain of these temptations, for we are forced to recognize that they are only the expression of the forces that were always hiding behind the facade of our supposed virtues. Dark things come out of the depths of our souls, and we have to consider them and recognize them for our own, and then repudiate them, lest we be saddled with them for eternity. Yet they return, and we cannot escape them. They plague us in our prayer. And while we face them, and cannot get rid of them, we realize more clearly than ever before our great need for God, and the tremendous debt we owe his honor, and we try to pray to him and it seems that we cannot pray. Then begins a spiritual re-evaluation of all that is in us. We begin to ask ourselves what is and is not *real* in our ideals!

This is the time when we really learn to pray in earnest. For now we are no longer proud enough to expect great lights and consolation in our prayer. We are satisfied with the driest crust of supernatural food, glad to get anything at all, surprised that God should even pay the slightest attention. And if we cannot pray (which is a source of concern) yet we know more than ever before how much we desire to pray. If we could be consoled at all, this would be our only consolation.

The man who cannot face such dryness and abandonment for a long time, with great patience, and ask nothing more of God but to do his holy will and never offend him, finally enters into pure prayer. Here the soul goes to God in prayer without any longer adverting either to itself or to its prayer. It speaks to him without knowing what it is saying because God himself has distracted the mind from its words and thoughts. It reaches him without thoughts because, before it can think of him, he is already present in the depths of the spirit, moving it to love him in a way it cannot explain or understand. Time no longer means anything in such prayer, which is carried on in instants of its own, instants that can last a second or an hour without our being able to distinguish one from another. For this prayer belongs less to time than to eternity.

This deep interior prayer comes to us of its own accord, that is, by the secret movement of the spirit of God, at all times and in all places, whether we be praying or not. It can come at work, in the middle of our daily business, at a meal, on a silent road, or in a busy thoroughfare, as well as at Mass, or in Church, or when we recite the psalms in choir. However, such prayer draws us naturally to interior and even exterior solitude. It does not depend on exterior conditions, but it has effected such an interior isolation and solitariness in our own souls that we naturally tend to seek silence and solitude for our bodies as well as for our souls. And it is good for the soul to be in solitude for a great part of the time. But if it should seek solitude for its own comfort and consolation, it will have to endure more darkness and more anguish and more trial. Pure prayer only takes possession of our hearts for good when we no longer desire any special light or grace or consolation for ourselves, and pray without any thought of our own satisfaction.

Finally, the purest prayer is something on which it is impossible to reflect until after it is over. And when the grace has gone we no longer seek to reflect on it, because we realize that it belongs to another order of things, and that it will be in some sense debased by our reflecting on it. Such prayer desires no witness, even the witness of our own souls. It seeks to keep itself entirely hidden in God. The experience remains in our spirit like a wound, like a scar that will not heal. But we do not reflect upon it. This living wound may become a source of knowledge, if we are to instruct others in the ways of prayer; or else it may become a bar and an obstacle to knowledge, a seal of silence set upon the soul, closing the way to words and thoughts, so that we can say nothing of it to other men. For the way is left open to God alone. This is like the door spoken of by Ezechiel, which shall remain closed because the King is enthroned within.

(No Man Is an Island, pp. 44–51)

Two Kinds of Wisdom

In the first two chapters of the first Epistle to the Corinthians St. Paul distinguishes between two kinds of wisdom: one which consists in the knowledge of words and statements, a rational, dialectical wisdom, and another which is at once a matter of paradox and of experience, and goes beyond the reach of reason. To attain to this spiritual wisdom, one must first be liberated from servile dependence on the "wisdom of speech." (1 Cor 1.17) This liberation is effected by the "word of the Cross" which makes no sense to those who cling to their own familiar views and habits of thought and is a means by which God "destroys the wisdom of the wise." (1 Cor 1.18–23) The word of the Cross is in fact completely baffling and disconcerting both to the Greeks with their philosophy and to the Jews with their well-interpreted Law. But when one has been freed from dependence on verbal formulas and conceptual structures, the Cross becomes a source of "power." This power emanates from the "foolishness of God" and it also makes use of "foolish instruments" (the Apostles). (1 Cor 1.27ff.) On the other hand, he who can accept this paradoxical "foolishness" experiences in himself a secret and mysterious power, which is the power of Christ living in him as the ground of a totally new life and a new being. (1 Cor 2.1–4, cf. Eph. 1.18–23, Gal. 6, 14–16)

Here it is essential to remember that for a Christian "the word of the Cross" is nothing theoretical, but a stark and existential experience of union with Christ in his death in order to share in his resurrection. To fully "hear" and "receive" the word of the Cross means much more than simple assent to the dogmatic proposition that Christ died for our sins. It means to be "nailed to the Cross with Christ," so that the ego-self is no longer the principle of our deepest actions, which now proceed from Christ living in us. "I live, now not I, but Christ lives in me." (Gal. 2.19–20; see also Romans 8.5–17) To receive the word of the Cross means the acceptance of a complete self-emptying, a *Kenosis*, in union with the self-emptying of Christ "obedient unto death." (Phil. 2.5–11) It is essential to true Christianity that this experience of the Cross and of self-emptying be central in the life of the Christian so that he may fully receive the Holy Spirit and know (again by experience) all the riches of God in and through Christ. (John 14.16–17, 26; 15.26–27; 16.7–15)

When Gabriel Marcel says: "There are thresholds which thought alone, left to itself, can never permit us to cross. An experience is required — an experience of poverty and sickness. . ." he is stating a simple Christian truth in terms familiar to Zen.

We must never forget that Christianity is much more than the intellectual acceptance of a religious message by a blind and submissive faith which never understands what the message means except in terms of authoritative interpretations handed down externally by experts in the name of the Church. On the contrary, faith is the door to the full inner life of the Church, a life which includes not only access to an authoritative teaching but above all to a deep personal experience which is at once unique and yet shared by the whole Body of Christ, in the Spirit of Christ. St. Paul compares this knowledge of God, in the Spirit, to the subjective knowledge that a man has of himself. Just as no one can know God except God's Spirit; yet this Holy Spirit is given to us, in such a way that God knows himself in us, and this experience is utterly real, though it cannot be communicated in terms understandable to those who do not share it. (See 1 Cor. 2.7–15) Consequently , St. Paul concludes, "we have the mind of Christ." (1 Cor. 2.16)

(*Thomas Merton on Zen*, pp. 112–114)

The True Human Personality

The root of personality is to be sought in the "true Self" which is manifested in the basic unification of consciousness in which subject and object are one. Hence the highest good is "the self's fusion with the highest reality." Human personality is regarded as the force which effects this fusion. The hopes and desires of the external, individual self are all, in fact, opposed to this higher unity. They are centered on the affirmation of the individual. It is only at the point where the hopes and fears of the individual self are done away with and forgotten "that the true human personality appears." In a word, realization of the human personality in this highest spiritual sense is for us the good toward which all life is to be oriented. It is even the "absolute good," insofar as the human personality is . . . intimately and probably even essentially related to the personality of God.

. . . the "deepest demand of man's heart" or the "religious demand" is the quest for a *personal* God. This demand does not lead to the ultimate satisfaction of individual aspirations: on the contrary, it requires their sacrifice and death. The individual self must cease to assert himself as a "center of unification" and of consciousness. God himself, the personal God, is the *deepest center* of consciousness and unification (remember the use of this expression by St John of the Cross). To fully realize this, not by quietistic annihilation and immersion but by the active and creative awareness of love, is our highest good.

(*Thomas Merton on Zen*, pp. 11)

Naked and Defenseless into the Center

If it is true that the deepest prayer at its nub is a perpetual surrender to God, then all meditation and specific acts of prayer might be seen as preparations and purifications to ready us for this never-ending yielding. Yet what is often conceded is that there is a terrible dread that sweeps over me in the face of such an expectation. If I am what I think myself to be and God is as I have pictured him to be, then perhaps I could bear to risk it. But what if he should turn out to be other than I have pictured him, and what if, in his piercing presence, whole layers of what I have known myself to be should dissolve away and an utterly unpredictable encounter should take place? Now we begin to face human dread —the dread that cloaks the unknown encounter of death — the dread that in miniature so often creates a crisis in a betrothal. We should let ourselves be brought naked and defenseless into the center of that dread where we stand alone before God in our nothingness without explanation, without theories, completely dependent upon his providential care, in dire need of the gift of his grace, his mercy and the light of faith. . . .

(*The Climate of Monastic Prayer*, p. 36)

Psychological Conscience:
Prayer is not the Place for Its Proper Development

One of the most important functions of the life of prayer is to deepen and strengthen and develop our moral conscience. The growth of our psychological conscience, although secondary, is not without importance also. The psychological conscience has its place in our prayer, but prayer is not the place for its proper development.

When we look inward and examine our psychological conscience our vision ends in ourselves. We become aware of our feelings, our inward activity, our thoughts, our judgments, and our desires. It is not healthy to be too constantly aware of all these things. Perpetual self-examination gives an overanxious attention to movements that should remain instinctive and unobserved. When we attend too much to ourselves, our activity becomes cramped and stumbling. We get so much in our own way that we soon paralyze ourselves completely and become unable to act like normal human beings.

It is best, therefore, to let the psychological conscience alone when we are at prayer. The less we tinker with it the better. The reason why so many religious people believe they cannot meditate is that they think meditation consists in having religious emotions, thoughts, or affections of which one is, oneself, acutely aware. As soon as they start to meditate, they begin to look into the psychological conscience to find out if they are experiencing anything worthwhile. They find little or nothing. They either strain themselves to produce some interior experience, or else they give up in disgust.

(*No Man Is an Island*, pp. 31–32)

The Divine Place within Things

Bios praktikos — *praxis* — the purification of the body, of the senses, of the passions — *apatheia* — the *puritas cordis* of John Cassian, something more than detachment, a positive openness to reality, to the Divine *Theoria physike* — a spiritual-ized knowledge of the created, a sort of natural contempla-tion, which does reach on to the divine *oikonomia*, God's plan for things, and the *logoi* of things, the divine place within things. At its highest it reaches to the contemplation of the spiritual *Theologia* — the contemplation of the Trinity without form or image.

It is by *theoria* that man helps Christ redeem the *logoi* of things and restore them to Himself. . . . The *theoria* is insepa-rable from love and from true spiritual conduct of life.

The "will of God" is no longer a blind force plunging through our lives like a cosmic steamroller and demanding to be accepted willy-nilly. On the contrary we are able to *under-stand* the hidden purpose of the creative wisdom and the divine mercy of God, and can cooperate with Him as a son with a loving Father. Not only that, but God himself hands over to man, when he is thus purified and enlightened, and united with the divine will, a certain creative initiative of his own, in political life, in art, in spiritual life, in worship; man is then endowed with a *causality* of his own.

(Unpublished Notes)

Expectancy for the Will of God

The life of infused contemplation does not always begin with a definite experience of God in a strong inpouring of light. Moments of freedom and escape from the blindness and helplessness of the ordinary, laborious ways of the spirit will always be relatively rare. And it is not too hard to recognize these sudden, intense flashes of the gifts of understanding, these vivid "rays of darkness" striking deep into the soul and changing the course of a man's whole life. They bring with them their own conviction. They strike blindness from our eyes like scales. They plant in us too deep and too calm and too new a certainty to be misunderstood or quickly forgotten.

But if a man had to wait for such experiences before he became a contemplative he might have to wait a long time — perhaps a whole lifetime. And perhaps his expectation would be vain.

It is more ordinary for the spirit to learn contemplation from God not in a sudden flash but imperceptibly, by very gradual steps. And as a matter of fact, without the ground-work of long and patient trial and slow progress in the dark-ness of pure faith, contemplation will never really be learned at all. For a few isolated, though intense, flashes of the spirit of understanding and wisdom will not make a man a contem-plative in the full sense of the word; contemplative prayer is only truly what it is called when it becomes more or less habitual. . . .

The mind finds itself entering uneasily into the shadows of a strange and silent night. The night is peaceful enough. But it is very strange. Thought becomes cramped and difficult. There is a peculiarly heavy sense of weariness and distaste for mental and spiritual activity. Yet at the same time the soul is haunted with a fear that this new impotence is a sin, or a sign of imperfection. It tries to force acts of thought and will. . . . Sometimes it makes a mad effort to squeeze some feeling of fervor out of itself, which is, incidentally, the worst thing it could possibly do. All the pretty images and concepts of God that it once cherished have vanished or have turned into unpleasant and frightening distortions. God is nowhere to be found. The words of prayers return in a hollow echo from the walls of this dead cave.

If a man in this night lets his spirit get carried away with fear or impatience and anxiety, he will come to a standstill. He will twist and turn and torture himself with attempts to see some light and feel some warmth and recapture the old consolations that are beyond recovery. And finally he will run away from darkness, and do the best he can to dope himself with the first light that comes along.

But there are others who, no matter how much they suffer perplexity and uneasiness in the wilderness where God begins to lead them, still feel drawn further and further on into the wasteland. They cannot think, they cannot meditate; their imagination tortures them with everything they do not want to see; their life of prayer is without light and without pleasure and without any feeling of devotion.

On the other hand they sense, by a kind of instinct, that peace lies in the heart of this darkness. Something prompts them to keep still, to trust in God, to be quiet and listen for his voice, to be patient and not to get excited. Soon they discover that all useless attempts to meditate only upset and disturb them; but at the same time, when they stay quiet in the muteness of naked faith, resting in a simple and open-eyed awareness, attentive to the darkness which baffles them, a subtle and indefinable peace begins to seep into their souls and occupies them with a deep and inexplicable satisfaction. This satisfaction is tenuous and dark. It cannot be grasped or identified. It slips out of focus and gets away. Yet it is there.

What is it? It is hard to say: but one feels that it is somehow summed up in "the will of God" or simply, "God."

The man who does not permit his spirit to be beaten down and upset by dryness and helplessness; but who lets God lead him peacefully through the wilderness and desires no other support or guidance than that of pure faith and trust in God alone will be brought to deep and peaceful union with him.

The man who is not afraid to abandon all his spiritual progress into the hands of God, to put prayer, virtue, merit, grace, and all gifts in the keeping of him from whom they all must come, will quickly be led to peace in union with him.

Just as the light of faith is darkness to the mind, so the supreme supernatural activity of the mind and will in contemplation and infused love at first seems to us like inaction. That is why our natural faculties are anxious and restless and refuse to keep still. They want to be the sole principals of their own acts. The thought they cannot act according to their own pleasure brings them a suffering and humiliation which they find it hard to stand.

But contemplation lifts us beyond the sphere of our natural powers.

When you are traveling in a plane close to the ground you realize that you are going somewhere; but in the stratosphere, although you may be going seven times at fast, you lose all sense of speed.

As soon as there is any reasonable indication that God is drawing the spirit into this way of contemplation, we ought to remain at peace in a prayer that is utterly simplified, stripped of acts and reflections and clean of images, waiting in emptiness and vigilant expectancy for the will of God to be done in us. This waiting should be without anxiety and without deliberate hunger for any experience that comes within the range of our knowledge or memory, because any experience that we can grasp or understand will be inadequate and unworthy of the state to which God wishes to bring our souls.

(*Seeds of Contemplation*, pp. 145–150)

The Essential Elements
of Mystical Contemplation

We are now in a position to summarize the essential elements of mystical contemplation.

1 — It is an intuition that on its lower level transcends the senses. On its higher level it transcends the intellect itself.

2 — Hence it is characterized by a quality of light in darkness, knowing in unknowing. It is beyond feeling, even beyond concepts.

3 — In this contact with God, in darkness, there must be a certain activity of love on both sides. On the side of the soul, there must be a withdrawal from attachment to sensible things, a liberation of the mind and imagination from all strong emotional and passionate clinging to sensible realities. "Passionate thinking" distorts our intellectual vision, preventing us from seeing things as they are. But also, we must go beyond intelligence itself and not be attached even to "simple (intuitive) thoughts." All thought, no matter how pure, is transcended in contemplation. The contemplative must then keep alert and detached from sensible and from even spiritual attachments. St. John of the Cross will teach us that the contemplative should turn away even from seemingly supernatural visions of God and of His saints, in order to remain in the darkness of unknowing. In any event, contemplation presupposes a generous and total effort of ascetic self-denial. But the final, ecstatic movement by which the contemplative "goes beyond" all things is passive, and beyond his own control.

4 — Contemplation is the work of love, and the contemplative proves his love by leaving all things, even the most

spiritual things, for God is nothingness, detachment and "night." But the deciding factor in contemplation is the free and unpredictable action of God. He alone can grant the gift of mystical grace and make Himself known by the secret, ineffable contact that reveals His presence in the depths of the soul. What counts is not the soul's love for God but God's love for the soul.

5 — This knowledge of God in unknowing is not intellectual, nor even in the strict sense affective. It is not the work of one faculty or another uniting the soul with an object outside itself. It is a work of interior union and of identification in divine charity. One knows God by becoming one with Him. One apprehends Him by becoming the object of His infinite mercies.

6 — Contemplation is a supernatural love and knowledge of God, simple and obscure, infused by Him into the summit of the soul, giving it a direct and experiential contact with Him.

Mystical contemplation is an intuition of God born of pure love. It is a gift of God that absolutely transcends all the natural capacities of the soul and which no man can acquire by any effort of his own. But God gives it to the soul in proportion as it is clean and emptied of all affections for things outside of Himself. In other words, it is God manifesting Himself, according to the promise of Christ, to those who love Him. Yet the love with which they love Him is also His gift; we only love Him because He has first loved us. We seek Him because He has already found us. *Ipse prior dilexit nos.* [He first loved us.]

But the thing that must be stressed is that *contemplation is itself a development and a perfection of pure charity*. He who loves God realizes that the greatest joy, the perfection of beatitude is to love God and renounce all things for the sake of God alone — or for the sake of love alone because God Himself is love. Contemplation is an intellectual experience of the fact that

God is infinite Love, that He has given Himself completely to us, and that from henceforth, love is all that matters.

7 — St. Bernard remarks that love is sufficient to itself, is its own end, its own merit, its own reward. It seeks no cause beyond itself and no fruit outside itself. The very act of loving is the greatest reward of love. To love with a pure, disinterested love the God Who is the source of all love can only be the purest and most perfect joy and the greatest of all rewards. *Amor praeter se non requirit causam, non fructum; fructum ejus, usus ejus.* [Love does not require any cause beyond itself, no fruit; its fruit, its exercise.] And he exclaims: "I love simply because I love, and I love in order to love." *Amo quia amo, amo ut amem.* (Sermon 83 on the Song of Songs)

8 — The experience of contemplative prayer, and the successive states of contemplation through which one passes, are all modified by the fact that the soul is passive, or partly passive, under the guidance of God. There is a special consolation in the sudden awareness and deep experiential conviction that one is being carried on or led away by the love of God. But there is also a special anguish in the acute sense of one's own helplessness and dereliction, when one is powerless to do anything for oneself. When our faculties can no longer serve us in their ordinary way, we are bound to pass through periods of strange incapacity, bitterness and even apparent despair. In either case, it would be best not to pay to much attention to the "phenomenon" one seems to be experiencing. Better to purify one's intention and refrain from self-analysis. The "depths" of dereliction and bitterness that surround us when we are out of our natural sphere, do not lend themselves to accurate observation. At such times, reflection on ourselves too easily becomes morbid or hypochondriacal. Faith, patience and obedience are the guides which must help us advance quietly in darkness without looking at ourselves.

As for the consolations of contemplative quietude: too intent a reflection on them quickly turns into a kind of narcissistic complacency and should be avoided. Even supposing that one is genuinely passive under the action of God (and some people are adept at imagining they are when this is not the case), still reflection on ourselves would be just the kind of activity that would prove an obstacle to the action of grace. The "ray of darkness" by which God enlightens our soul in passive contemplation has this about it: that it makes us indifferent to ourselves, to our spiritual ambitions, and to our own "state." If we let the light of God play on the depth of our souls in its own way, and refrain from too much curious self-introspection, we will gradually cease to worry about ourselves, and forget these useless questions. This indifference and trust is itself a mystic grace, a gift of Divine Counsel, that leaves all decisions to God in the wordlessness of a present that knows no explanations, no projects and no plans. As Eckhart says, mystical love of God is a "love that asks no questions."

9 — Contemplation is the light of God playing directly upon the soul. But every soul is weakened and blinded by the attachments to created things, which it tends to love inordinately by reason of original sin. Consequently, the light of God affects that soul the way the light of the sun affects a diseased eye. It causes *pain*. God's love is too pure. The soul, impure and diseased, weakened by its own selfishness, is shocked and repelled by the very purity of God. It cannot understand the suffering caused by the light of God. It has formed its own ideas of God: ideas that are based upon natural knowledge and which unconsciously flatter self-love. But God contradicts those ideas. His light rejects all the natural notions the soul has formed for itself concerning Him. The experience of God in infused contemplation is a flat contradiction of all the soul has imagined about Him. The fire of His infused love

carries out a merciless attack upon the self-love of the soul attached to human consolations and to those lights and feelings which it required as a beginner, but which it falsely imagined to be the great graces of prayer.

10 — Infused contemplation, then, sooner or later brings with it a terrible interior revolution. Gone is the sweetness of prayer. Meditation becomes impossible, even hateful. Liturgical functions seem to be an insupportable burden. The mind cannot think. The will seems unable to love. The interior life is filled with darkness and dryness and pain. The soul is tempted to think that all is over and that, in punishment for its infidelities, all spiritual life has come to an end.

This is a crucial point in the life of prayer. It is very often here that souls called by God to contemplation, are repelled by this "hard saying," turn back and "walk no more with Him." (John vi, 61–67) God has illuminated their hearts with a ray of His light. But because they are blinded by its intensity it proves to be, for them, *a ray of darkness*. They rebel against that. They do not want to *believe* and remain in obscurity: they want to *see*. They do not want to walk in emptiness, with blind trust: they want to know where they are going. They want to be able to depend on themselves. They want to trust their own minds and their own wills, their own judgments and their own decisions. They want to be their own guides. They are therefore sensual men, who "do not perceive the things that are of the Spirit of God." To them, this darkness and helplessness is foolishness. Christ has given them His Cross and it has proved to be a scandal. They can go no further.

Generally they remain faithful to God: they try to serve Him. But they turn away from interior things and express their service in externals. They externalize themselves in pious practices, or they immerse themselves in work in order to escape the pain and sense of defeat they have experienced in what seems, to them, to be the collapse of all contemplation.

The light shineth in darkness and the darkness did not comprehend it. (John 1, 5)

(*The Inner Experience*, pp. 72–76)

The Signs of Infused Prayer

The first sign of infused prayer is then this inexplicable and undaunted seeking, this quest that is not put off by aridity, or darkness, or frustration. On the contrary, in deepest darkness it finds peace, and in suffering it does not lack joy. Pure faith and blind hope are enough. Clear knowledge is not necessary. . . . seeking Him blindly, undauntedly, in spite of dryness, in spite of the apparent hopelessness and irrationality of the quest, is then the first sign that this pre-experiential contemplation may be infused. Another sign would be the forgetfulness of ordinary cares and of the routine level of life, in the darkness of prayer. Though the contemplative seeking for God may seem in a way quite senseless, yet in the depths of our soul it makes a great deal of sense, while on the other hand the seemingly rational preoccupations and projects of normal life now appear to be quite meaningless. This is important, because as a matter of fact a quite similar sense of meaninglessness is now prevalent everywhere, and more or less affects every intelligent man. Not that everyone who feels the futility of life is *ipso facto* a contemplative. But the fact that secular existence has begun to clearly manifest its own meaninglessness to everyone with eyes to see, enables all sensitive and intelligent people to experience something akin to one of the phases of pre-contemplative purification. They can profit by this to learn a very healthy and fruitful spiritual detachment.

Finally, a third sign that pre-experiential contemplation may have an infused character is the very definite and powerful sense of attraction which holds the soul prisoner in mystery. Although the soul is filled with a sense of affliction and defeat, *it has no desire to escape from this aridity*. Far from being attracted by legitimate pleasures and lights and relaxations of the natural order, it finds them repellent. All created goods only make it restless. They cannot satisfy it. Even spiritual consolations have lost their appeal and become tedious. But at the same time there is a growing conviction that joy and peace and fulfillment are only to be found somewhere in this lonely night of aridity and faith.

Sometimes this attraction is so powerful that it cancels out all the suffering felt by the soul, which counts its own pain and helplessness as nothing and becomes totally absorbed in this inexplicable desire for peace which it thinks can somehow be found in solitude and darkness. It follows the attraction, or rather allows itself to be drawn through the night of faith by the power of an obscure love which it cannot yet understand.

Then suddenly comes the awakening to a new level of experience.

The soul one day begins to realize, in a manner completely unexpected and surprising, that in this darkness it has found the living God. It is overwhelmed with the sense that He is there and that His love is surrounding and absorbing it on all sides. In fact, He has been there all the time — but He was utterly unknown. Now He is recognized. At that instant, there is no other important reality but God, infinite Love. Nothing else matters. The darkness remains as dark as ever and yet, somehow, it seems to have become brighter than noonday. The soul has entered a new world, a world of rich experience that transcends the level of all other knowledge and all other love.

From then on its whole life is transformed. Although externally sufferings and difficulties and labors may be multiplied, the soul's interior life has become completely simple. It consists of one thought, one preoccupation, one love: GOD ALONE. In all things the eyes of the soul are upon Him. And this gaze of the soul includes in itself all adoration, all petition; it is continual sacrifice, it offers God unceasing reparation. It is perfect prayer, perfect worship. It is pure and simple love, that love which, as St. Bernard says, draws and absorbs every other activity of the soul into itself: *Amor caeteros in se omnes traducit et captivat affectus.* (Sermon 83 on the Song of Songs) This love, infused into the soul by God, unifies all its powers and raises them up to Him, separating its desires and affections more and more from the world and from perishing things. Without realizing it, the soul makes rapid progress and becomes free, virtuous and strong: but it does not consider itself. It has no eyes for anything or anyone but God alone.

It has entered into the maturity of the spiritual life, the illuminative way, and is being drawn on towards complete union with God.

(*The Inner Experience*, pp. 86–88)

A Contemplative Spirituality
Centered in the Mystery of Marriage

If you are waiting for someone to come along and feed you the contemplative life with a spoon, you are going to wait a long time, especially in America. You had better renounce your inertia, pray for a little imagination, ask the Lord to awaken your creative freedom, and consider some of the following possibilities:

1) It is possible that by the sacrifice of seemingly good economic opportunities you could move into the country or to a small town where you would have more time to think. This would involve the acceptance of a relative poverty perhaps. If so, all the better for your interior life. The sacrifice could be a real liberation from the pitiless struggle which is the source of most of your worries. There are of course jobs which by their nature keep one isolated, or take him off the beaten track. However, not everyone is free to choose the career of forest ranger or lighthouse keeper. Not everybody wants to spend his life as a night watchman, and for very good reasons. But what is wrong with farming?

2) Wherever you may be, it is always possible to give yourself the benefit of those parts of the day which are quiet because the world does not value them. One of these is the small hours of the morning. Even when a man cannot put a few hundred miles between himself and the city, if he can get up around four or five in the morning he will have the whole place to himself, and taste something of the peace of solitude. Besides, the dawn is by its very nature a peaceful, mysterious and contemplative time of day — a time when one naturally pauses and looks with awe at the eastern sky. It is a time of new life, new beginning and therefore important to the spiritual life: for the spiritual life is nothing else but a perpetual interior renewal. To go to early Mass is always preferable, even though the later Masses may be more splendid and solemn. At the early Mass, things are quieter, more sober, more austere. The poor go to early Mass, because they have to get to work sooner. And Christ is more truly with the poor. His spiritual presence among them makes *their* Mass the more contemplative.

3) It should be too obvious to mention, that Sunday is set apart by nature and by the tradition of the Church as a day of contemplation. Puritan custom tended to make Sunday seem

a negative sort of "sabbath" characterized most of all by the things one "must not" do. The inevitable reaction against this stressed the legitimate, but more or less insignificant, recreations that make Sunday a day of rest for the body as well as for the spirit. Obviously, if you sleep all Sunday morning you are missing something about the day of rest that is more important than bodily sleep. Sunday is a day of contemplation not because it is a day without work, a day when the shops and banks and offices are closed. But because it is sacred to the mystery of the resurrection. Sunday is the "Lord's Day" not in the sense that, on one day out of the week, one must stop and think of Him, but because it breaks into the ceaseless, "secular" round of time with a burst of light out of a sacred eternity. We stop working and rushing about on Sunday not only in order to rest up and start over again on Monday but in order to collect our wits and realize the relative meaninglessness of the secular business which fills the other six days of the week, and taste the satisfaction of a peace which surpasses understanding and which is given us by Christ. Sunday reminds us of the peace that should filter through the whole week when our work is properly oriented. Sunday is a contemplative day not just because Church Law demands that every Christian assist at Mass, but because everyone, Christian or not, who celebrates the day spiritually and accepts it at its face value, opens his heart to the light of Christ, the light of the resurrection. In so doing he grows in love, in faith, and is able to "see" a little more of the mystery of Christ. He certainly may have no clear idea of what is happening, but the grace of God produces its effects in his heart. Sunday then is a day of grace, a day of light, in which light is given. Simple fidelity to this obvious duty, realization of this gift of God, will certainly help the harassed layman to take his first steps on the path to a kind of contemplation.

4) Whenever one seeks the light of contemplation, he commits himself by that very fact to a certain spiritual discipline. This is just as true outside the cloister as in it. But it would be a mistake for a man or woman with all the obligations and hardships of secular life to live in the world like a cloistered monk. To try to do this would be an illusion. The first sacrifice of the lay contemplative living in the world is his acceptance of the fact that he is *not* a monk and, consequently, of the fact that his prayer life must be correspondingly humble and poor. Active virtue and good works play a large part in the "contemplative" life that is led in the world, and the uncloistered man of prayer is most likely to be what we have called a "masked contemplative." It will only do him harm if, tormented by his thirst for a clearer and higher experience, he tries to force the issue and advance his "degree of prayer" by violent and ill-considered efforts.

The discipline of the contemplative in the world is first of all the discipline of fidelity to his duty of state — to his obligations as head of a family, as member of a profession, as a citizen. This discipline, these duties can demand very great sacrifices. Perhaps indeed some of the difficulties of people in the world exact of them far greater sacrifice than they would find in the cloister. In any case, their contemplative life will be deepened and elevated by the depth of their understanding of their duties. Here too, mere conformism and lip-service are not enough. It is not sufficient to "be a good Catholic." One must penetrate the inner meaning of his life in Christ and see the full significance of its demands. One must carry out his obligations not as a question of form, but with a real, personal decision to offer the good he does to God, in and through Christ. The virtue of a Christian is something creative and spiritual, not simply a fulfillment of a law. It must be penetrated and filled with the "newness," the Christlikeness, which comes from the action of the Spirit of God in his heart, and which elevates his smallest good act to an entirely spiritual level. Needless to say, this is more than a matter of verbalizing one's "purity of intention."

5) It follows from this that for the married Christian, his married life is essentially bound up with his contemplation. This is inevitable. It is by his marriage that he is situated in the mystery of Christ. It is by his marriage that he bears witness to Christ's love for the world, and in his marriage that he experiences that love. His marriage is a sacramental center from which grace radiates out into every department of his life, and consequently it is his marriage that will enable his work, his leisure, his sacrifices and even his distractions to become in some degree contemplative. For by his marriage all these things are ordered to Christ and centered in Christ.

It should above all be emphasized that for the married Christian, even and especially married love enters into his contemplation, and this, as a matter of fact, gives it a special character.

The union of man and wife in nuptial love is a sacred and symbolic act, the very nature of which signifies the mystery of the union of God and man in Christ. Now this mystery is the very heart and substance of contemplation. Hence, married love is a kind of material and symbolic expression of man's desire for God and God's desire for man. It is a blind, simple groping way of expressing man's need to be utterly and completely *one*. It is a childlike acting out of division of man in himself and of his hunger for union with his other self. The Greek Fathers thought that before the Fall Adam and Eve were really and literally two *in one flesh*, that is to say they were one single being. That human nature, united with God, was whole and complete in itself. But after the fall man was divided into two and thereafter sought by sexual love to recover his lost unity. But this desire is ever frustrated by original sin. The fruit of sexual love is not perfection, not completeness, but only the birth of another Adam or another Eve, frail, exiled, incomplete. The child in turn grows to manhood, and, devoured by the old yearning for completeness, marries, reiterates the dark mystery of love and hopelessness, brings forth new beings to incompleteness and frustration, and finally dies incomplete.

But the coming of Christ has exorcised the futility and despair of the children of Adam. Christ has married human nature, united man and God in Himself, in one Person. In Christ, the completeness we were born for is realized. In Him there is no longer marrying or giving in marriage. But in Him all are one in the perfection of charity.

Pius XII pointed out in the Encyclical *Sacra Virginitas* that the state of Christian virginity, with its pure love, attaining to contemplation, lays hold on the reality and substance of that union with God which married love imperfectly attempts to symbolize. Therefore the virginal state is more perfect, because contemplation is more germane to it, and theoretically inseparable from it. However, married love, in its more humble and more earthly way may in fact be, for the enlightened layman, a more concrete and sensible approach to the great mystery. He lays hold on his lost unity in that secret mystery of sorrow and ecstasy, humiliation and joy, triumph and death, which is his own peculiar participation in the mystery of Christ.

Hence it is clear that for the married Christian layman, contemplation does not involve the discipline and attitudes proper to a virgin. The married Christian should beware of letting himself be influenced too much by a virginal or priestly spirituality that has nothing to do with his state and only blinds him to its essential dignity. There are in fact too many books which look at the spiritual life exclusively from the standpoint of a virginal or priestly life, and their needless multiplication is, in fact, the reason why there is so much sterile spiritual writing. At the same time, this sterile influence makes itself felt in the interior life of those married Christians who should have the greatest influence for good in keeping the Christian mind fully and sanely *incarnate*.

In conclusion, then, though it is right that the Christian layman try to keep his life ordered and peaceful, and to some extent recollected, what he needs most of all is a contemplative spirituality centered in the mystery of marriage. The development of such a spirituality is very necessary and much to be desired.

(*The Inner Experience*, pp. 137–141)

The Concerned Monk
at the Heart of the World

After having learned about *theoria physike* and having been brought truly into the experience of it by his experience on the corner of Fourth and Walnut in March of 1958, Merton now listened to the world in a new way. Rather than rejecting it with all its sinfulness, which he identified so much with his own sinful past, he now embraced it with something of the loving compassion of Christ, the Savior of all. He saw how men and women were more sinned against than sinners, and even as sinners were the beloved of God, whom the Son was sent to heal and make whole. A righteous anger began to burn within him, not directed toward any person or persons, but toward the institutional evil, the deep prejudices, the effects of sin in us. These are the forces that violate and seek to degrade and dehumanize the human person. He saw them at work blatantly in the recent past in the holocaust and in all out warfare, ultimately expressed in the use of the atomic bomb but continuing into his present time in Vietnam. He saw it painfully present all around him in the way Afro-Americans and Native Americans, as were indigenous people everywhere, being mistreated even by supposedly good Christians. In his compassion he spoke out, in poetry and in prose.

In this section we offer a few samples from his prose pieces. Merton speaks out positively as well as negatively. He not only condemns the evil but he calls us all to positive action to change things and amend these crimes against humanity, against our own human person.

I Do not Consider Myself Integrated in the War-Making Society

I do not consider myself integrated in the war-making society in which I live, but the problem is that this society *does* consider *me* integrated in it. . . . I have been simply living where I am and developing in my own way without consulting the public about it since it is none of the public's business.

(Day of a Stranger, p. 15)

The Hermit Life Is Cool

The hermit life is cool. It is a life of low definition in which there is little to decide, in which there are few transactions or none, in which there are no packages to be delivered. In which I do not bundle up packages and deliver them to myself. It is not intense. There is no give and take of questions and answers, problems and solutions. Problems begin down the hill. Over there under the water tower are the solutions. Here there are woods, foxes. Here there is no need for dark glasses. "Here" does not even warm itself up with references to "there." It is just a "here" for which there is no "there." The hermit life is that cool. . . .

This is not a hermitage — it is a house. ("Who was that hermitage I seen you with last night?. . .") What I wear is pants. What I do is live. How I pray is breathe. Who said Zen? Wash out your mouth if you said Zen. If you see a meditation going by, shoot it. Who said "Love"? Love is in the movies. The spiritual life is something that people worry about when they are so busy with something else they think they ought to be spiritual. Spiritual life is guilt. Up here in the woods is seen the New Testament: that is to say, the wind comes through the trees and you breathe it. Is it supposed to be clear? I am not inviting anybody to try it. Or suggesting that one day the message will come saying NOW. That is none of my business.

I am out of bed at two fifteen in the morning, when the night is darkest and most silent. Perhaps this is due to some ailment or other. I find myself in the primordial lostness of night, solitude, forest, peace, a mind awake in the dark, looking for a light, not totally reconciled to being out of bed. A light appears, and in the light an icon. There is in the large darkness a small room of radiance with psalms in it. The psalms grow up silently by themselves without effort like plants in this light which is favorable to them. The plants hold themselves up on stems which have a single consistency, that of mercy, or rather great mercy. *Magna misericordia.* In the formlessness of night and silence a word then pronounces itself: Mercy. It is surrounded by other words of lesser consequence: "destroy iniquity" "wash me" "purify" "I know my iniquity." *Peccavi.* Concepts without interest in the world of business, war, politics, culture, etc. Concepts also often without interest to ecclesiastics.

Other words: Blood. Guile. Anger. The way that is not good. The way of blood, guile, anger, war.

Out there the hills in the dark lie southward. The way over the hills is blood, guile, dark, anger, death: Selma, Birmingham, Mississippi. Nearer than these, the atomic city, from which each day a freight car of fissionable material is brought to be laid carefully beside the gold in the underground vault which is at the heart of the nation.

"Their mouth is the opening of the grave; their tongues are set in motion by lies; their heart is void."

Blood, lies, fire, hate, the opening of graves, void. Mercy, great mercy.

The birds begin to wake. It will soon be dawn. In an hour or two the towns will wake, and men will enjoy everywhere the great humorous smile of production and business.

(*Day of a Stranger*, pp. 37–45)

Day of a Stranger

Rituals. Washing out the coffee pot in the rain bucket. Approaching the outhouse with circumspection on account of the king snake who likes to curl up on one of the beams inside. Addressing the possible king snake in the outhouse and informing him that he should not be there. Asking the formal ritual question that is asked at this time every morning: "Are you in there, you bastard?"

More rituals. Spray bedroom (cockroaches and mosquitoes). Close all the windows on south side (heat). Leave windows open on north and east sides (cool). Leave windows open on west side until maybe June when it gets very hot on all sides. Pull down shades. Get water bottle. Rosary. Watch. Library book to be returned.

It is time to visit the human race.

I start out under the pines. The valley is already hot. Machines out there in the bottoms, perhaps planting corn. Fragrance of the woods. Cool west wind under the oaks. Here is the place on the path where I killed a copperhead. There is the place where I saw the fox run daintily and carefully for cover carrying a rabbit in his mouth. And there is the cement cross that, for no reason, the novices rescued from the corner of a destroyed wall and put up in the woods: people imagine someone is buried there. It is just a cross. Why should there not be a cement cross by itself in the middle of the woods?

A squirrel is kidding around somewhere overhead in mid-air. Tree to tree. The coquetry of flight.

I come out into the open over the hot hollow and the old sheep barn. Over there is the monastery, bugging with windows, humming with action. . . .

I climb sweating into the novitiate, and put down my water bottle on the cement floor. The bell is ringing. I have duties, obligations, since here I am a monk. When I have accomplished these, I return to the woods where I am nobody. In the choir are the young monks, patient, serene, with very clear eyes, then, reflective, gentle, confused. Today perhaps I tell them of Eliot's *Little Gidding,* analyzing the first movement of the poem ("Midwinter spring is its own season"). They will listen with attention thinking that some other person is talking to them about some other poem. . . .

In the refectory is read a message of the Pope, denouncing war, denouncing the bombing of civilians, reprisals on civilians, killing of hostages, torturing of prisoners (all in Vietnam). Do the people of this country realize who the Pope is talking about? They have by now become so solidly convinced that the Pope never denounces anybody but Communists that they have long since ceased to listen. The monks seem to know. The voice of the reader trembles.

In the heat of noon I return with the water bottle freshly filled, through the cornfield, past the barn under the oaks, up the hill, under the pines, to the hot cabin. Larks rise out of the long grass singing, A bumblebee hums under the wide shady eaves.

I sit in the cool back room, where words cease to resound, where meanings are absorbed in the *consonance* of heat, fragrant pine, quiet wind, bird song and one central tonic note that is unheard and unuttered. This is no longer time of obligations. In the silence of the afternoon all is present and all is inscrutable in one central tonic note to which every other sound ascends or descends, to which every other meaning aspires, in order to find its true fulfillment. To ask when the note will sound is to lose the afternoon: it has already sounded, and all things now hum with the resonance of it sounding.

I sweep. I spread a blanket out in the sun. I cut grass behind the cabin. I write in the heat of the afternoon. Soon I will bring the blanket in again and make the bed. The sun is over clouded. The day declines. Perhaps there will be rain. A bell rings in the monastery. A devout Cistercian tractor growls in the valley. Soon I will cut bread, eat supper, say psalms, sit in the back room as the sun sets, as the birds sing outside the window, as night descends on the valley. I become surrounded once again by all the silent Tzu's and Fu's (men without office and without obligation). The birds draw closer to their nests. I sit on the cool straw mat on the floor, considering the bed in which I will presently sleep alone under the icon of the Nativity.

Meanwhile the metal cherub of the apocalypse passes over me in the clouds, treasuring its egg and its message.

(*Day of a Stranger*, pp. 53–63)

I Have Heard the Voice of All the Hemisphere

I cannot be a "North American" who knows only the rivers, the plains, the mountains and the cities of the north, the north where already there are no Indians, where the land was colonized and cultivated by Puritans where, under the audacious and sarcastic splendor of the skyscrapers, one rarely sees the Cross and where the Holy Virgin, when she is represented at all, is pale and melancholy and carries no Child in her arms. . . . It seems to me that I have heard the voice of all the hemisphere in the silence of my monastery, a voice that speaks from the depth of my being, with a clarity at once magnificent and terrible: as if I had in the depths of my heart the vast and solitary pampas, the brilliant hoarfrost of the Bolivian plateau, the thin air of the terraced valleys of the Incas, the splendor and suavity of Quito, the cold plains of Bogota, and the intolerably mysterious jungles of the Amazon.

(*Day of a Stranger*, p. 14)

I Decided to Marry the Silence

One might say I had decided to marry the silence of the forest. The sweet dark warmth of the whole world will have to be my wife. Out of the heart of that dark warmth comes the secret that is heard only in silence, but it is the root of all the secrets that are whispered by all the lovers in their beds all over the world. So perhaps I have an obligation to preserve the stillness, the silence, the poverty, the virginal point of pure nothingness which is at the center of all other loves. I attempt to cultivate this plant without comment in the middle of the night and water it with psalms and prophecies in silence. It becomes the most rare of all the trees in the garden, at once the primordial paradise tree, the *axis mundi*, the cosmic axle, and the Cross. *Nulla silva talem profert*. There is only one such tree. It cannot be multiplied. It is not interesting.

(*Day of a Stranger*, p. 49)

Non-Cooperation with Injustice,
Disorder and Untruth

Some of the most characteristic and least understood elements in Gandhi's non-violent mystique follow from this principle which implies a rejection of the basic idea of the affluent industrial society. A society that lives by organized greed or by systematic terrorism and oppression (they come to much the same thing in the end) will always tend to be violent because it is in a state of persistent disorder and moral confusion. The first principle of valid political action in such a society then becomes *non-cooperation* with its disorder, its injustices, and more particularly with its deep commitment to untruth.

Satyagraha is meaningless if it is not based on the awareness of profound inner contradiction in all societies based on force. "It is not possible for a modern state based on force non-violently to resist forces of disorder, whether external or internal." Hence *satyagraha* according to Gandhi cannot seriously accept claims advanced by a basically violent society that hopes to preserve order and peace by the threat of maximum destruction and total hate. *Satyagraha* must begin by putting itself against this claim in order that the seriousness of one's dedication to truth may be put to the test. It is not possible for the truly non-violent man simply to ignore the inherent falsity and inner contradictions of a violent society. On the contrary, it is for him a religious and human duty to confront the untruth in that society with his own witness in order that the falsity may become evident to everyone. The first job of a *satyagrahi* is to bring the real situation to light even if he has to suffer and die in order that injustice be unmasked and appear for what it really is.

All the political acts of Gandhi were, then, at the same time spiritual and religious acts in fulfillment of the Hindu *dharma*.

They were meaningful on at least three different levels at once: first as acts of religious worship, second as symbolic and educative acts bringing the Indian people to a realization of their true needs and their place in the life of the world, and finally they had a universal import as manifestations of urgent truths, the unmasking of political falsehood, awakening all men to the demands of the time and to the need for renewal and unity on a world scale.

(*Gandhi on Non-Violence*, pp. 9–10)

Their Rightful Integrity as Persons

It is very well to insist that man is a "social animal" — the fact is obvious enough. But that is no justification for making him a mere cog in a totalitarian machine — or in a religious one either, for that matter.

In actual fact, society depends for its existence on the inviolable personal solitude of its members. Society, to merit its name, must be made up not of numbers, but of persons. To be a person implies responsibility and freedom, and both these imply a certain interior solitude, a sense of personal integrity, a sense of one's own reality and of one's ability to give himself to society — or to refuse that gift.

When men are merely submerged in a mass of impersonal human beings pushed around by automatic forces, they lose their capacity for self-determination. When society is made up of men who know no interior solitude it can no longer be held together by love; and consequently it is held together by a violent and abusive authority. But when men are violently deprived of the solitude and freedom which are their due, the society in which they live becomes putrid; it festers with servility, resentment and hate.

No amount of technological progress will cure the hatred that eats away the vitals of materialistic society like a spiritual cancer. The only cure is, and must always be, spiritual. There is not much use talking to men about God and love if they are not able to listen. The ears with which one hears the message of the Gospel are hidden in man's heart, and these ears do not hear anything unless they are favored with a certain interior solitude and silence.

In other words, since faith is a matter of freedom and self-determination — the free receiving of a freely given gift of grace — man cannot assent to a spiritual message as long as his mind and heart are enslaved by automatism. He will always remain so enslaved as long as he is submerged in a mass of other automatons, without individuality and without their rightful integrity as persons.

(*Thoughts in Solitude*, pp. 12–14)

A Schizoid Society

The white man, says Laurens Van Der Post, came into Africa (and Asia and America for that matter) like a one-eyed giant, bringing with him the characteristic split and blindness which were at once his strength, his torment, and his ruin. With his self-isolated and self-scrutinizing individual mind, Western man was master of concepts and abstractions. He was the king of quantity and the driver of those forces over which quantitative knowledge gave him supremacy without understanding. Because he ruled matter without understanding it, he faced his bodily self as an object which he could not comprehend though he could analyze and tamper with its every part. He submitted to passions which, though he no longer regarded them as devils, were nevertheless inscrutable and objective forces flying at him from the dark outside the little circle illumined by a pragmatic and self-complacent moral reason. The one-eyed giant had science without wisdom, and he broke in upon ancient civilizations which (like the medieval West) had wisdom without science: wisdom which transcends and unites, wisdom which dwells in body and soul together and which, more by means of myth, of rite, of contemplation, than by scientific experiment, opens the door to a life in which the individual is not lost in the cosmos and in society but found in them. Wisdom which made all life sacred and meaningful — even that which later ages came to call secular and profane.

It is true that neither the ancient wisdoms nor the modern sciences are complete in themselves. They do not stand alone. They call for one another. Wisdom without science is unable to penetrate the full sapiential meaning of the created and material cosmos. Science without wisdom leaves men enslaved to a world of unrelated objects in which there is no way of discovering (or creating) order and deep significance in man's own pointless existence. The vocation of modern man was to bring about their union in preparation for a new age. The marriage was wrecked on the rocks of the white man's dualism and of the inertia, the incomprehension, of ancient and primitive societies. We enter the post-modern (perhaps the post-historic!) era in total disunity and confusion. But while the white man has always, naturally, blamed the traditional ancient cultures and the primitive "savage" whom he never understood, it is certainly clear that if the union of science and wisdom has so far not been successful it is not because the East would not listen to the West; the East has been all too willing to listen. The West has not been able to listen to the East, to Africa, and to the now practically extinct voice of primitive America. As a result of this the ancient wisdoms have themselves fallen into disrepute and Asia no longer dares listen to herself!

The split of the European mind has become universal. All men (says L. L. Whyte) are caught in the "fundamental division between deliberate activity organized by static concepts, and the instinctive and spontaneous life." This dissociation, which was fruitful in the Renaissance, has now reached a point of mad development, of "behavior patterns unrelated to organic needs" and a "relentless passion for quantity" . . . "Uncontrolled industrialism and excess of analytic thought" . . . "without the catharsis of rhythmic relaxation or satisfying achievement."

> This [Whyte continues] is the moment of uninhibited perversions which can now ally themselves with technical power . . . in a brief period of dominance. This short reign of Antichrist depends on the fusion of two principles which are both vicious because they represent only a past of European or Western human nature: instinctive vitality distorted into sadism, and differentiating human vitality distorted into quantitive expansion.

Whyte was writing this in the days of Hitler, Mussolini, and Stalin, at the beginning of the Second World War. The "short" reign of Antichrist would soon, he believed, give way to a reign of light, peace, harmony, and reconstruction. The end of the war would begin a better era. Or at least so he hoped, though not without reservation, for he added: "one more dark decade would disprove my judgment, revealing a rot deeper than I have seen." We are now in the third dark decade since his words were written.

Ananda Coomaraswamy, writing about the same time as L. L. Whyte, viewed the sickness of civilization in more religious terms, and with much the same seriousness. The problem of the whole world was the problem of Western man: for everywhere the one spiritual illness was now rampant, and malignancies, which in the West were perhaps endemic, were proliferating in the most alarming fashion in the East and in Africa.

"East and West," Coomaraswamy wrote, "are at cross purpose only because the West is determined, i.e., at once resolved and economically 'determined,' to keep on going it knows not where, and it calls the rudderless voyage 'Progress.'"

He wrote before the days of Red China and of postwar Japan, both of which now lead scores of other nations in carrying the logic of the Western split to its most extreme dissociation. Today it is not only the West that is "determined" on its rudderless voyage; all, down to the newest African nation, are in the same centrifugal flight, and the itinerary points to outer space.

The question remains the same. It is a crisis of *sanity* first of all. The problems of the nations are the problems of mentally deranged people, but magnified a thousand times because they have the full, straight-faced approbation of a schizoid society, schizoid national structures, schizoid military and business complexes, and, need one add, schizoid religious sects. "We are at war with ourselves," said Coomaraswamy, "and therefore at war with one another. Western man is unbalanced, and the question, Can he recover himself? is a very real one."

The question is all the more urgent now that it concerns not only Western man but everybody.

There have of course been spurious attempts to bring East and West together. One need not review all the infatuated theosophies of the nineteenth century. Nor need one bother to criticize the laughable syncretisms which have occupied the talents of publicists (more often Eastern than Western) in which Jesus, Buddha, Confucius, Tolstoy, Marx, Nietzsche, and anyone else you like join in the cosmic dance which turns out to be not Shiva's but just anybody's. However, the comparison of Eastern and Western religious philosophy is, in our time, reaching a certain level of seriousness and this is one small and hopeful sign. The materials for a synthesis of science and wisdom are not lacking.

(*Gandhi on Non-Violence*, pp. 1–3)

Invented Identities

In defining and limiting the Indian as we have, we are also expressing a definition and limitation within ourselves. In putting the Indian under tutelage to our own supposedly superior generosity and intelligence, we are in fact defining our inhumanity, our own insensitivity, our own blindness to human values. In effect, how is the Indian defined and hemmed in by the relationship we have imposed on him? His reservation existence — somewhat like the existence of an orphan in an asylum — is as close to non-existence as we can get him without annihilating him altogether. I fully realize that this will arouse instant protest. The Indian is not confined to his reservation: he has another choice. He is free to raise himself up, to get out and improve his lot, to make himself human, and how? Why, of course, by joining us, by doing as we do, by manifesting business acumen and American know-how, by making money, and by being integrated into our affluent society. Very generous indeed.

But let us spell out quite what this means. IT MEANS THAT AS FAR AS WE ARE CONCERNED THE INDIAN (LIKE THE NEGRO, THE ASIAN, ETC.) IS PERMITTED TO HAVE A HUMAN IDENTITY ONLY

INSOFAR AS HE CONFORMS TO OURSELVES AND TAKES UPON HIM-SELF OUR IDENTITY. But since in fact the Indian, or the Negro, is in the position of having different colored skin and other traits which make him unlike ourselves, he can never be like us and can therefore never have an identity. The lock snaps shut. The Indian, like the Negro (though perhaps less emphatically), is definitely excluded. He can never sell himself to us as fully human on our impossible terms. In theory we recognize his humanity. In practice he is, like the Negro, at best a second-class human who tries to dress and act like ourselves but never quite manages to make the grade. Therefore "Indians are now principally on the reservation." They have failed to establish themselves in society, "But" and we continue to paraphrase, "placing them on reservations was an act to protect white settlers from psychological depredations, from any loss of self-esteem by an admission that the Indians might be hum-anly equals. To protect white America from the realization that the Indian was not an inferior being. In order to guar-antee that the Indian conformed to the white man's idea of him, the Indian was more and more deprived of his original holdings, since for the white man identity is coextensive with the capacity to own property, to have holdings, and to make a lot of money."

In one word, the ultimate violence which the American white man, like the European white man, has exerted in all unconscious "good faith" upon the colored races of the earth (and above all on the Negro) has been to impose on them *invented identities*. To place them in positions of subservience and helplessness in which they themselves came to believe only in the identities which had thus been conferred upon them.

The ultimate surrender of the Indian is to believe himself a being who belongs on a reservation or in an Indian ghetto, and to remain there without identity, with the possible but generally unreal option of dreaming that he *might* find a place in white society. In the same way the ultimate defeat of the Negro is for him to believe that he is a being who belongs in Harlem, occasionally dreaming that if only he could make it to Park Avenue he would at last become real.

(Ishi Means Man, pp. 9–11)

They Were Considered Subhuman

Genocide is a new word. Perhaps the word is new because technology has now got into the game of destroying whole races at once. The destruction of races is not new — just easier. Nor is it a specialty of totalitarian regimes. We have forgotten that a century ago white America was engaged in the destruction of entire tribes and ethnic groups of Indians. The trauma of California gold. And the vigilantes who, in spite of every plea from Washington for restraint and understanding, repeatedly took matters into their own hands and went out slaughtering Indians. Indiscriminate destruction of the "good" along with the "bad" — just so long as they were Indians. Parties of riffraff from the mining camps and saloons suddenly constituted themselves defenders of civilization. They not only combed the woods and canyons — they even went into the barns and ranch houses, to find and destroy the Indian servants and hired people, in spite of the protests of the ranchers who employed them.

The Yana Indians (including the Yahi or Mill Creeks) lived around the foothills of Mount Lassen, east of the Sacramento River. Their country came within a few miles of Vina where the Trappist monastery in California stands today. These hill tribes were less easy to subdue than their valley neighbors. More courageous and more aloof, they tried to keep clear of the white man altogether. They were not necessarily more ferocious than other Indians, but because they kept to themselves and had a legendary reputation as "fighters," they were more feared. They were understood to be completely "savage." As they were driven further and further back into the hills, and as their traditional hunting grounds gradually narrowed and emptied of game, they had to raid the ranches in order to keep alive. White reprisals were to be expected, and they were ruthless. The Indians defended themselves by guerilla warfare. The whites decided that there could be no peaceful coexistence with such neighbors. The Yahi, or Mill Creek Indians, as they were called, were marked for complete destruction. Hence they were regarded as subhuman. Against them there were no restrictions and no rules. No treaties need be made for no Indian could be trusted. Where was the point in "negotiation"?

Ishi, the last survivor of the Mill Creek Indians, whose story was published by the University of California at Berkeley in 1964, was born during the war of extermination against his people. The fact that the last Mill Creeks were able to go into hiding and to survive for another fifty years in their woods and canyons is extraordinary enough. But the courage, the resourcefulness, and the sheer nobility of these few stone age men struggling to preserve their life, their autonomy and their identity as a people rises to the level of tragic myth. Yet there is nothing mythical about it. The story is told with impeccable objectivity — though also with compassion — by the scholars who finally saved Ishi and learned from him his language, his culture, and his tribal history. . . .

"They have separated murder into two parts and fastened the worse on me" — words which William Carlos Williams put on the lips of a Viking Exile, Eric the Red. Men are always separating murder into two parts: one which is unholy and unclean: for "the enemy," another which is a sacred duty: "for our side." He who first makes the separation, in order that he may kill, proves his bad faith. So too in the Indian wars. Why do we always assume the Indian was the aggressor? We were in *his* country, we were taking it over for ourselves and we likewise refused even to share any of it with him. We were the people of God, always in the right, following a manifest destiny. The Indian could only be a devil. But once we allow ourselves to see all sides of the question, the familiar perspectives of American history undergo a change. The "savages" suddenly become human and the "whites," the "civilized," can seem barbarians. True, the Indians were often cruel and inhuman (some more than others). True also, the humanity, the intelligence, the compassion and understanding which Ishi met with in his friends the scholars, when he came to join our civilization, restore the balance in our favor. But we are left with a deep sense of guilt and shame. The record is there. The Mill Creek Indians, who were once seen as bloodthirsty devils, were peaceful, innocent and deeply wronged human beings. In their use of violence they were, so it seems, generally very fair. It is we who were the wanton murders, and they who were the innocent victims. The loving kindness lavished on Ishi in the end did nothing to change that fact. His race had been barbarously, pointlessly destroyed. . . .

One cannot help thinking today of the Vietnam war in terms of the Indian wars of a hundred years ago. Here again, one meets the same myths and misunderstandings, the same obsession with "completely wiping out" an enemy regarded as diabolical. The language of the Vigilantes had overtones of puritanism in it. The backwoods had to be "completely cleaned out," or "purified" of Indians — as if they were vermin. I have read accounts of American GI's taking the same attitude toward the Vietcong. The jungles are thought to be "infested" with communists, and hence one goes after them as one would go after ants in the kitchen back home.

And in this process of "cleaning up" (the language of "cleansing" appeases and pacifies the conscience), one becomes without realizing it a murderer of women and children. But this is an unfortunate accident, what the moralists call "double effect." Something that is just too bad, but which must be accepted in view of something more important that has to be done. And so there is more and more killing of civilians and less and less of the "something more important" which is what we are trying to achieve. In the end, it is the civilians that are killed in the ordinary course of events, and combatants only get killed by accident. No one worries any more about double effect. War is waged against the innocent to "break enemy morale."

(*Ishi Means Man*, pp. 25–32)

The Good Must Be Recaptured
Over and Over Again

All forms of necessity can contribute to man's freedom. There is material and economic need. There is spiritual need. The greatest of man's spiritual needs is the need to be delivered from the evil and falsity that are in himself and in his society. Tyranny, which makes a sagacious use of every human need and indeed artificially creates more of them in order to exploit them all to the limit, recognizes the importance of guilt. And modern tyrannies have all explicitly or implicitly in one way or another emphasized the *irreversibility of evil* in order to build their power upon it.

For instance, it is not unusual in all political life, whether totalitarian or democratic, to incriminate the political novice in order to test his mettle and make sure of his commitment. He must be willing to get his hands dirty, and if he is not willing he must be framed so that he will have a record that can, when necessary, be used against him. Then he will be a committed man. He will henceforth cooperate with acts which might have given him pause if he were not himself marked with guilt. Who is he to complain of certain shady actions, certain discreet deals, certain white lies, when he knows what it is in his file at headquarters?

It is no accident that Hitler believed firmly in the unforgivableness of sin. This is indeed fundamental to the whole mentality of Nazism, with its avidity for final solutions and its concern that all uncertainties be eliminated.

Hitler's world was built on the central dogma of the irreversibility of evil. Just as there could be no quarter for the Jews, so the acts that eliminated them were equally irreversible and there could really be no excuse for the Nazis themselves. Even the arguments of an Eichmann, pleading obedience, suggest deep faith in an irreversible order which could not be changed but only obeyed. Such was the finality of Hitler's acts and orders that all the trials of all the Nazis who have been caught, whether they have been executed or liberated or put in prison for short terms, have changed absolutely nothing. It is clear that Hitler was in one thing a brilliant success: everything he did bears the stamp of complete paranoid finality. . . .

A belief in the finality and irreversibility of evil implies a refusal to accept the precarious and the risk that attend all finite good in this life. Indeed, the good that men do is always in the realm of the uncertain and of the fluid, because the needs and sufferings of men, the sins and failures of men, are constant, and love triumphs, at least in this life, not by eliminating evil once for all but by resisting and overcoming it anew every day. The good is not assured once for all by one heroic act. It must be recaptured over and over again. St. Peter looked for a limit to forgiveness. Seven times, and then the sin was irreversible! But Christ told him that forgiveness must be repeated over and over again, without end.

(*Gandhi on Non-Violence*, pp. 11–13)

Non-Violence Seeks to Change Relationships

The "fabric" of society is not finished. It is always "in becoming." It is on the loom, and it is made up of constantly changing relationships. Non-violence takes account precisely of this dynamic and non-final state of all relationships among men, for non-violence seeks to change relationships that are evil into others that are good, or at least less bad.

Hence non-violence implies a kind of bravery far different from violence. In the use of force, one simplifies the situation by assuming that the evil to be overcome is clear-cut, definite, and irreversible. Hence there remains but one thing: to eliminate it. Any dialogue with the sinner, any question of the irreversibility of his act, only means faltering and failure. Failure to eliminate evil is itself a defeat. Anything that even remotely risks such defeat is in itself capitulation to evil. The irreversibility of evil then reaches out to contaminate *even the tolerant thought* of the hesitant crusader who, momentarily, doubts the total evil of the enemy he is about to eliminate.

Such tolerance is already complicity and guilt, and must be eliminated in its turn. As soon as it is detected it becomes irreversible.

Fortitude, then, equals fanaticism. It grows with unreason. Reasoning itself is by its very nature tinged with betrayal.

Conscience does indeed make cowards. It makes Judases. Conscience must be eliminated.

This is the familiar mental machinery of tyrannical oppression. But reducing necessities to simple and irreversible forms it simplifies existence, eliminating questions that tend to embarrass minds and slacken the "progress" of the relentless and intolerant apparatus. Sin is thus prevented from entering into the living dialectic of society. And yet a dialectic that ignores the presence of evil is itself bad because it is untrue. The greatest of tyrannies are all therefore based on the postulate that *there should never be any sin*. That therefore what happened either was not a sin ("Dallas has no sin," as we all were quasi-officially informed at the end of 1963) or else it has been immediately wiped out (by a lynch mob, or a Jack Ruby). Since sin is what should never be, then it must never be, therefore *it will never be*. The most awful tyranny is that of the proximate Utopia where the last sins are currently being eliminated and where, tomorrow, there will be no more sins because all the sinners will have been wiped out.

> Non-violence has a different logic. It recognizes that sin is an everyday occurrence which is in the very nature of action's constant establishment of new relationships within a web of relations, and it needs forgiving, dismissing, in order to make it possible for life to go on by constantly releasing men from what they have done unknowingly. Only through this constant mutual release from what they do can men remain free agents, only by their constant willingness to change their minds and start again can they be trusted with so great a power as that to begin something new.

This remarkable statement of Hannah Arendt's shows the inherent relation between non-violence and the renewal of India for which Gandhi lived and died. A violent change would not have been a serious change at all. To punish and destroy the oppressor is merely to initiate a new cycle of violence and oppression. The only real liberation is that which *liberates both the oppressor and the oppressed* at the same time from the same tyrannical automatism of the violent process which contains in itself the curse of irreversibility. "The freedom contained in Jesus' teaching of forgiveness is the *freedom from vengeance*, which encloses both doer and sufferer in the relentless automatism of the action process, which by itself need never come to an end."

True freedom then is inseparable from the inner strength which can assume the common burden of evil which weighs both on oneself and one's adversary. False freedom is only a manifestation of the weakness that cannot bear even one's own evil until it is projected onto the other and seen exclusively his. The highest form of spiritual freedom is, as Gandhi believed, to be sought in the strength of heart which is capable of liberating the oppressed and the oppressor together. But in any event the oppressed must be able to be free within himself, so that he may begin to gain strength to pity his oppressor. Without that capacity for pity, neither of them will be able to recognize the truth of their situation: a common relationship in a common complex of sins.

(*Gandhi on Non-Violence*, p. 5)

The Only Way Truly to "Overcome" an Enemy

When asked if it was lawful to overcome force with force, Erasmus answered that this might be permissible according to "Imperial laws" but he wondered how it would be relevant for a Christian, who is bound to follow the law of Christ,

> granted that human laws do not punish what they permitted. Yet what is Christ your leader going to

do if you defraud this law. . . . If your enemy is
hungry, give him to eat. . . . In so doing you will
heap coals of fire upon his head, that is to say, you
will enkindle the fire of love in him.

To the objection that rendering good for evil only lays one
open to greater evil, Erasmus replied:

If you can avoid evil by suffering it yourself, do so.
Try to help your enemy by overcoming him with
kindness and meekness. If this does not help, then
it is better that one perish than both of you. It is
better that you be enriched with the advantage of
patience than to render evil for evil. It is not enough
to practice the golden rule in this matter. The
greater your position the more ready you ought to
be to forgive another's crime.

Here, as usual in Erasmus, one finds no platitudes. The apparently simple suggestion that one can avoid evil by suffering it
contains an arresting paradox. One can overcome evil by taking it upon oneself, whereas if one flies from it he is not certain to escape and may, even if he seems to escape, be
overwhelmed. The only way truly to "overcome" an enemy is
to help him become other than an enemy. This is the kind of
wisdom we find in Gandhi. It is the wisdom of the Gospels.

It is also the wisdom of the Apostolic Fathers. We read in
the *Shepherd of Hermas*:

For, if you are long-suffering, the Holy Spirit
dwelling in you will be clear, unobscured by any
other spirit of evil. Dwelling in a spacious place, he
will rejoice and be glad with the lodging in which he
finds himself. Thus, he will serve God with abun-
dant cheerfulness, because he has his well-being

within himself. However, if violent anger enters, the good spirit in his sensitiveness is immediately confined, since he has not a clean habitation. So, he tries to withdraw from the place. . . . For, the Lord dwells amid longsuffering, but the devil has his abode in anger. . . . Take a little wormwood and pour it into a jar of honey. Is not the honey spoiled altogether? Even a great quantity of honey is ruined by the smallest amount of wormwood and its sweetness is lost. It is no longer pleasant to the owner, because it has been mixed and it is no longer enjoyable. Now, if no wormwood is put into the honey, it turns out to be sweet and becomes useful to the owner. You see, then, that long-suffering is very sweet, far more than honey, and useful to the Lord. His dwelling is in long-suffering. . . .

The evils we suffer cannot be eliminated by violent attack in which one sector of humanity flies at another in destructive fury. Our evils are common and the solution of them can only be common.

(*Gandhi on Non-Violence*, pp. 15–16)

The First Duty of Every Man Is to Return to His Own "Right Mind"

The first duty of every man is to return to his own "right mind" in order that society may be sane.

Coomaraswamy, in an important article ["On Being in One's Right Mind," *Review of Religion,* November, 1942], once outlined the meaning of the process called *metanoia*, or recovery of one's right mind, the passage from ignorance of self to enlightened moral awareness. "Repentance," he said, quoting Hermas, "is a great undertaking" (and by no means an emotional crisis!). It is the ability to cast off the intolerable burden of the past act, no longer seen as irreversible. But obviously no man enclosed in himself can utter an omnipotent word of command and abolish his own sin. The "knowledge" and "understanding" which is truly the "great [and repentant, liberated] understanding" is therefore "understanding-with" or "*con*-scientia" (conscience). "A kind of synthesis or agreement by which our internal conflict is resolved and 'all the knots of the heart are loosed.' " It is to understand "with" our inmost self *in a union transcending consciousness of a within or a without.*

This is obviously something much deeper than a mere interiority or a form of pious and introverted recollection. It is supraconscious and suprapersonal. And it obviously implies the ability to come into unity with the *prajnatman* (the solar spirit), or what the Greek Fathers would call the *pneuma*.

We find St. Thomas speaking somewhat in these terms in an interesting question in the *Summa* on blindness of mind. There is, he says, a principle of intellectual vision in man, and man can give his attention to this principle or turn away from it. He turns away either by willful refusal to acknowledge its authority, or by becoming absorbed in the love of other things which he prefers to the intellectual light. And St. Thomas quotes Psalm 57:9 — *Fire hath fallen on them* (the fire of desire) *and they shall not see the sun.*

The *Shepherd of Hermas* speaks of the Spirit of Truth as a trust given by God to man, living and dwelling in him in order to be returned to the Lord undefiled by any lie. "Love truth and let nothing but the truth issue from your mouth, in order that the spirit which God has settled in this flesh of yours may be found truthful in the sight of men. . . . Liars ignore the Lord and defraud him since they do not return the Spirit received from him, namely a Spirit in which there is no lie." Hearing this, Hermas weeps and declares: "I have not yet spoken a true word in all my life!" And the Angel then tells him that this declaration is the beginning of truth in himself. Of course in this context truth and forgiveness go together, and there must be *one* truth and one forgiveness both for myself and my brothers. Both truth and mercy are falsified when I judge by a double standard.

The capacity for forgiveness and for understanding in this highest sense makes men able to transcend the limitation of that self which is the subject of evil, St. Cyprian says, "If no one can be without sin . . . how necessary and how beneficent is divine clemency which, since it recognizes that even those who are healed still retain some wounds, has granted health-giving remedies to be used in curing the wounds that remain to be healed." But this is not a merely mental operation, a manipulation of "pure intentions" and the excitation of subjective benevolence toward offenders. It means an immo-lation of one's empirical self, by mercy and sacrifice, in order to save and liberate oneself and the other. Coomaraswamy here quotes the *Maitri Upanishad*: "When the mind has been immolated in its own source for love of truth, then the false controls of actions done when it was deluded by sensibilia likewise pass away." This is the mystical basis of Gandhi's doctrine of freedom in truth as end, and of *satyagraha* (the vow of truth) as the means of attaining the end. Coomaraswamy also quotes a few lines from Jakob Boehme which throw light on this idea which is, of course, fundamentally Christian. Boehme says:

> Thou shalt do nothing but forsake thy own will, viz., that which thou callest "I" or "thyself." By which means all thy evil properties will grow weak, faint and ready to die, then thou wilt sink down

again into that one thing from which thou art origi-
nally sprung.

To forgive others and to forget their offense is to enter with
them into the healing mystery of death and resurrection in
Christ, to return to the source of the Spirit which is the Heart
of Christ. And by this forgiveness we are ourselves cleansed:
Unde vulneratus fueras, inde curare [Let that by which you were
wounded become your own cure], says Cyprian.

It should be quite obvious that *satyagraha* has nothing in it
of Western middle-class banality. It does not mean "honesty
is the best policy," because it is far more than honesty and
it is infinitely more than a policy. One does not obey the
prajnatman, or intellectual principle, the "spirit of truth,"
simply in order to get something out of one's obedience.

The truth may turn out in terms of the current moods and
trends of a blind society to be supremely unprofitable. In that
case, when truth becomes absolutely the worst policy, one
follows it anyway, even when it leads to death.

(*Gandhi on Non-Violence*, pp. 16–18)

Keep Me in This Silence

To be here with the silence of Sonship in my heart is to be a
center in which all things converge upon you. That is surely
enough for the time being. Therefore, Father, I beg you to keep
me in this silence so that I may learn from it the word of your
peace and the word of your mercy and the word of your
gentleness to the world. And that through me perhaps your
word of peace may make itself heard where it has not been
possible for anyone to hear it for a long time.

(*Conjectures of a Guilty Bystander* p. 178)

The Later Poetry

Young Merton heard a taunting voice:
    "Tomorrow, tomorrow Death will come
    And find you sitting dumb and senseless
    With your epics unbegun. . . ."
Merton's later poetry and poetic prose pieces like *Original Child Bomb*, give voice, often heart-rending voice, to the social concerns that filled his later years. There are also beautiful pieces like *Hagia Sophia*. But his epics were not left "unbegun." *Cables to the Ace* and *The Geography of Lograire* are exceedingly curious works, the latter considered still incomplete by the author. They contain many elements which reflect the searching and strivings of the man who began to write "antipoems." "In this wide-angle mosaic of poems and dreams I have without scruple mixed what is my own experience with what is almost everybody else's," writes Merton of *Lograire*, "And where more drastic editing is called for by my own dream, well, I have dreamed it."

And the Children of Birmingham

And the children of Birmingham
Walked into the story
Of Grandma's pointed teeth
("Better to love you with")

Reasonable citizens
Rose to exhort them all:
"Return at once to schools of friendship.
But in stores of love and law."

(And tales were told
Of man's best friend, the Law.)
And the children of Birmingham
Walked in the shadow
Of Grandma's devil
Smack up against
The singing wall,
Fire and water
Poured over everyone:
"Hymns were extreme,
So there could be no pardon!"

And old Grandma
Began the lesson
Of everybody's skin,
Everybody's fun:
"Liberty may bite
An irresponsible race
Forever singing,"
Grandma said,
"Forever making love:
Look at all the children!"

(And tales were told
Of man's best friend, the Law.)

And the children of Birmingham
Walked into the fury
Of Grandma's hug:

Her friendly cells
("Better to love you with.")
Her friendly officers
And "dooms of love."

Laws had a very long day
And all were weary.

But what the children did that time
Gave their town
A name to be remembered!

(And tales were told
Of man's best friend, the Law.)

(The Collected Poems, 335–337)

Picture of a Black Child with a White Doll
Carole Denise McNair, Killed in Birmingham, September 1963

Your dark eyes will never need to understand
Our sadness who see you
Hold that plastic glass-eyed
Merchandise as if our empty-headed race
Worthless full of fury
Twanging and drooling in the southern night
With guns and phantoms
Needed to know love

(Yet how deep the wound and the need
And how far down our hell

Are questions you need not
Answer now)

That senseless platinum head
Of a hot city cupid
Not yet grown to whore's estate
It glories and is dull
Next to your live and lovely shape
Your smile and your person
Yet that silly manufactured head
Would soon kill you if it could think
Others as empty do and will
For no reason
Except for the need
Which you know without malice
And by a bitter instinct
The need for love.

So without a thought
Of death or fear
Of night
You glow full of dark ripe August
Risen and Christian
Africa purchased
For the one lovable Father alone.

And what was ever darkest and most frail
Was then your treasure-child
So never mind
They found you and made you a winner
Even in most senseless cruelty
Your darkness and childhood
Became fortune yes became
Irreversible luck and halo.   (*Collected Poems*, pp. 626f)

The Guns of Fort Knox

Guns at the camp (I hear them suddenly)
Guns make the little houses jump. I feel
Explosions in my feet, through boards.
Wars work under the floor. Wars dance in the foundations.
    Trees
Must also feel the guns they do not want
Even in their core.
As each charge bumps the shocked earth
They shudder from the root.

Shock the hills, you guns! They are
Not too firm even without dynamite.
These Chinese clayfoot hills
Founded in their own shale
Shift their feet in friable stone.

Such ruins cannot
Keep the armies of the dead
From starting up again.
They'll hear these guns tonight
Tomorrow or some other time.
They'll wake. They'll rise
Through the stunned rocks, form
Regiments and do death's work once more.

Guns, I say, this is not
The right resurrection. All day long
You punch the doors of death to wake
A slain generation. Let them lie
Still. Let them sleep on,
O Guns. Shake no more

(But leave the locks secure)
Hell's door.

(*Collected Poems*, pp. 228f)

Original Child Bomb

32: The bomb exploded within 100 feet of the aiming point. The fireball was 18,000 feet across. The temperature at the center of the fireball was 100,000,000 degrees. The people who were near the center became nothing. The whole city was blown to bits and the ruins all caught fire instantly everywhere, burning briskly. 70,000 people were killed right away or died within a few hours. Those who did not die at once suffered great pain. Few of them were soldiers.

33: The men in the plane perceived that the raid had been successful, but they thought of the people in the city and they were not perfectly happy. Some felt they had done wrong. But in any case they had obeyed orders. "It was war." . . .

38: On August 9th another bomb was dropped on Nagasaki, though Hiroshima was still burning. . . .

40: As to the Original Child that was now born, President Truman summed up the philosophy of the situation in a few words. "We found the bomb" he said "and we used it."

41: Since that summer many other bombs have been "found." What is going to happen? At the time of writing, after a season of brisk speculation, men seem to be fatigued by the whole question.

(*Collected Poems*, pp. 300ff)

Paper Cranes

(The Hibakusha come to Gethsemani)
How can we tell a paper bird
Is stronger than a hawk
When it has no metal for talons?
It needs no power to kill
Because it is not hungry.
Wilder and wiser than eagles
It ranges round the world
Without enemies
And free of cravings.

The child's hand
Folding these wings
Wins no wars and ends them all.

Thoughts of a child's heart
Without care, without weapons!
So the child's eye
Gives life to what it loves
Kind as the innocent sun
And lovelier than all dragons!

(*Collected Poems*, p. 740)

April 4th 1968

For Martin Luther King

On a rainy night
On a rainy night in April
When everybody ran
Said the minister

On a balcony
Of a hotel in Tennessee
"We came at once
Upstairs"

On a night
On a rainy night in April
When the shot was fired
Said the minister

"We came at once upstairs
And found him lying
After the tornado
On the balcony
We came at once upstairs"

On a rainy night
He was our hope
and we found a tornado
Said the minister.

And a well-dressed white man
Said the minister.
Dropped the telescopic storm

And he ran
(The well-dressed minister of death)
He ran
He ran away

And on the balcony
Said the minister
We found
Everybody dying   (*Collected Poems*, pp. 1005f)

Hagia Sophia

I. *Dawn. The Hour of Lauds*

There is in all visible things an invisible fecundity, a dimmed light, a meek namelessness, a hidden wholeness. This mysterious Unity and Integrity is Wisdom, the Mother of all, *Natura naturans*. There is in all things an inexhaustible humility. This is at once my own being, my own nature, and the Gift of my Creator's Thought and Art within me, speaking as Hagia Sophia, speaking as my sister, Wisdom.

I am awakened, I am born again at the voice of this my Sister, sent to me from the depths of the divine fecundity.

Let us suppose I am a man lying in a hospital. I am indeed this man lying asleep. It is July the second, the Feast of Our Lady's Visitation. A Feast of Wisdom.

At five-thirty in the morning I am dreaming in a very quiet room when a soft voice awakens me from my dream. I am like all mankind awakening from all the dreams that ever were dreamed in all the nights of the world. It is like the One Christ awakening in all the separate selves that ever were separate and isolated and alone in all the lands of the earth. It is like all minds coming back together into awareness from all distractions, cross-purposes and confusions, into unity of love. It is like the first morning of the world (when Adam, at the sweet voice of Wisdom awoke from nonentity and knew her), and like the last morning of the world when all the fragments of Adam will return from death at the voice of Hagia Sophia and will know where they stand.

Such is the awakening of one man, one morning at the voice of a nurse in the hospital. Awakening out of languor and darkness, out of helplessness, out of sleep, newly confronting reality and finding it to be gentleness.

It is like being awakened by Eve. It is like being awakened by the Blessed Virgin. It is like coming forth from primordial nothingness and standing in clarity, in Paradise.

In the cool hand of the nurse there is the touch of all life, the touch of Spirit.

Thus Wisdom cries out to all who will hear (*Sapientia clamitat in plateis*) and she cries out particularly to the little, to the ignorant and the helpless. . . .

(*Collected Poems*, pp. 363f)

Antipoem I

O gentle fool
He fell in love
With the electric light
Do you not know, fool
That love is dynamite?

Keep to what is yours
Do not interfere
With the established law
    See the dizzy victims of romance
Unhappy moths!

Please observe
This ill-wondered troth.

All the authorities
In silence anywhere
Swear you only love your mind
If you marry a hot wire.

Obstinate fool
What a future we face
If one and all
Follow your theology
You owe the human race
An abject apology.   (*Collected Poems*, pp. 671f)

Cables to the Ace
or
Familiar Liturgies of Misunderstanding

Prologue
    You, Reader, need no prologue. Do you think these Horatian Odes are all about you? Far from the new wine to need a bundle. You are no bundle. Go advertize yourself.
    Why not more pictures? Why not more rhythms, melody, etc.? All suitable to be answered some other time. The realm of spirit is two doors down the hall. There you can obtain more soul than you are ready to cope with, Buster.
    The poet has not announced these mosaics on purpose. Furthermore he has changed his address and his poetics are on vacation.
    He is not roaring in the old tunnel.
    Go shake hands with the comics if you demand a preface. My attitudes are common and my ironies are no less usual

than the bright pages of your favorite magazine. The soaps, the smells, the liquors, the insurance, the third, dull, gin-soaked cheer: what more do you want, Rabble?
    Go write your own prologue.
I am the incarnation of everybody and the zones of
    reassurance.
I am the obstetrician of good fortune. I live in the social cages
    of joy.
It is morning, afternoon or evening, Begin.
I too have slept here in my stolen Cadillac.
I too have understudied the Paradise swan.

Each ant has his appointed task
One to study strategy
And one to teach it
One to cool the frigidaire
And one to heat it.

Each ant has his appointed round
In the technical circuit
All the way to high
One to make it and the other to brake it.

And each has his appointed vector
In the mathematical takeoff
In the space-supported dance
The comedy of orders.

And each must know the number of his key
With a key in his eye and an eye for numbers
A number of appointments
A truly legal score:
And each must find his logical apartment.

Each ant had his appointed strategy to heat
To fuse and to fire at the enemy
And cool it down again to ninety-nine
In the right order —
But sometimes with the wrong apparatus.

It rained dark and cold on the Day of St. Theresa of the Heart
For no one yet knew that it was holiday fifteen
It rained like weather in honor of her sacred love
For the notables had built a black stone wall around her heart
And the prelates, mayors, and confessors wanted the doors
    closed.
The tongue of her heart, they said, must proffer insults
    to the vision.
So they built four walls of cold rain around the vision.
And the rain came down upon the vision in honor of her love.
In the theological cell where she was locked alone with the
    vision
Her heart was pierced by a thousand needles of fire.
Then the mayors, prelates, and confessors all wept together
    in honor of her love.
They went together in procession to the rainy city walls and
    fortified
Their minds, wrapping them in the folds of the black storm.
Behind them in the invisible town the jails and convents
    overflowed with flame.
In the smallest window of all St. Theresa
Forgotten by these entranced jokers turned her heat into
    a dove.
The rain ended at that moment.
The dove had flown into the fiery center of the vision.

(Collected Poems, pp. 396, 430, 450)

Geography of Lograire

Author's Note

This is a purely tentative first draft of a longer work in progress in which there are, necessarily, many gaps. This is only a beginning of patterns, the first opening up of the dream. A poet spends his life in repeated projects, over and over again attempting to build or to dream the world in which he lives. . . .

In this wide-angle mosaic of poems and dreams I have without scruple mixed what is my own experience with what is almost everybody else's. Thus "Cargo" and "Ghost Dance," for instance, cease to be bizarre anomalies and are experienced as yours and mine as well as "theirs." . . .

Much also has been found in the common area of nightmare to which we are all vulnerable (advertising, news, etc.). The most personally subjective part is perhaps the long meditation on Eros and Thanatos, centering in the New York City Borough of Queens [where Merton lived with his parents and later with his grandparents], in the "North" canto.

Prologue: The Endless Inscription

1. Long note one wood thrush hear him love in waste pine
        places
    Slow doors all ways of ables open late
    Tarhead unshaven the captain signals
    Should we wait?

2. Down wind and down rain and down mist the passenger.

3. In holy ways there is never so much must. . . .

15. Plain Savior crosses heaven on a pipe

16. Hay Abraham fennel and grass rain ram under span's star
    Red grow the razors in the Spanish hollow

17. Gallow my Savior the workless sparrow
    Closes my old gate on dead tar's ira slam
    gone far summer too far fret work blood
    Work blood and tire tar under light wood
      Night way plain home to wear death down hard
      Ire hard down on anger heel grind home down
      Wary is smashed cotton-head beaten down mouth
      When will they all go where those white Cains are dead?

18. Sign Redeemer's "R"
    Buys Mars his last war.

III. Cargo Songs

1. Sir William MacGregor
   Representative of her Majesty the Queen
   Saw the Paramount Chief enthroned
   On a high platform
   Went up and seized him by the hair
   Dragged him to the ground
   Placed himself firmly in the seat of honor: "No one shall
   sit higher in Papua than I."

2. The anthropologist lay low
   Shivered under the hot compress
   Read Bronte and pissed black
   When the wind blew off the sea
   He thought he felt better
   Seemed to hear the bell-charm of St. Martin's
   And Strand traffic humming in his head
   Lay thinking of French chophouses in Soho

Of anything in fact
But Trobriand Islanders and coral gardens
Even his intimate fantasies were far away
In Russia: Rasputin: a convenient system!
"How wicked I am," sighed the anthropologist,
"I need more quinine
And no one shall sit higher in Trobriand than I."

3. Meanwhile four natives must hang
   Each in a different village
   To impress the population
   The proceedings throughout
   Were watched with great interest
   By chiefs and a number
   Of other natives
   All appeared impressed
   By the solemnity.

4. Hatedevil missionary has a waxen smell
   Long narrow trousers find their way to hell
   Rams chickens forbidden Kava and the vices
   Of a river god seen between trees
   An old man with a forgettable name
   Lights volcano nine.
   The Captain notes odd behavior and shivers.

5. Even though
   The anthropologist is laid low
   There is still nobody higher.

6. After this a native from the North side of Milna Bay
   Possessed by a tree-spirit
   Warned of giant waves
   All must throw away
   Matches, knives, white men's tools

Destroy houses kill all pigs
Withdraw inland
Wearing only long narrow leaves
"To show entire repudiation of the white man."

7. On the following Sunday the missionary noted with surprise that his congregation now consisted only of a few children. He learned that the villagers were all in the hills, expecting the return of the dead. He pushed inland without further delay. He found all the men of the village sitting in tense silence. His cordial greeting met with no reply.

8. But the missionary had come prepared:

"I had in my wallet a long thin stick of trade to-bacco, a delicacy very much prized by these people, and as I was sitting in the doorway of the Chief's house I took it out and threw it to some men who were sitting behind me in the dark. Almost before they had time to pick it up it came back and struck me in the ear." (*Rev. Abel*)

9. The whites then made for safety moving fast in small groups to the coast. They reached the boats in time. The dead arrived in the village with a cargo of flashlights.

10. Now there is a black King living in the jungle. . . .

III. Ghost Dance: Prologue

American horse Fast Thunder spotted
Horse pretty back good lance present
Nov 27 1890

    We were made many promises by the Commissioners but
we never heard from them since.
    They talked nice to us and after we signed they took our
land cut down our rations.
    They made us believe we would get full sacks if we signed
but instead our sacks are empty.
    Our chickens were all stolen our cattle were killed our crops
were entirely lost because we were absent talking with the
Commission.
    We were told if we do as white men do we will be better off
but we are getting worse off every year.

When we were in Washington the President
The Secretary the Commissioner promised

We would get back a million lbs. of beef
Taken from us and the Bill
Passed Congress
But the Commissioner
Refused
To give us
Any meat.

IV. Ghost Dance

1. All the old time prophecies about the whites coming to this country and about guns have come true so what we have dreamed about the end is probably true as well. . . .

(*Collected Poems*, pp. 457ff)

Humorous Verse

Cheese

Joyce Killer-Diller

I think that we should never freeze
Such lively assets as our cheese:
The sucker's hungry mouth is pressed
Against the cheese's caraway breast

A cheese, whose scent like sweet perfume
Pervades the house through every room.

A cheese that may at Christmas wear
A suit of cellophane underwear,

Upon whose bosom is a label,
Whose habitat:—The Tower of Babel.

Poems are nought but warmed-up breeze,
Dollars are made by Trappist Cheese.

Psalm 132: A Modern Monastic Revision
David ben Jungfreud

Ecce quam leve et quam jocosum
Cruciari fratres in Capitulo!

Ave cadaveres laniatos filiorum Cain!
O jucunda nimis clamor praelii
O delicata confusio tremendi comercii!

Surgit Sadiusiste, percutit baculo
Manu, pede, hic illic, nimis ardenter!

Immolat fratres Sadius gaudens, necnon Masoch
Vult vapulare, vult, et participat!

Die felix Purgatorium noctu exultans
Animas devorat!

Ah! What a thrill it is for us all,

descendants of Adam —
by way of Cain and the Marquis of Sade—

to dwell together
and kick each other into heaven,

while Leopold von Sacher-Masoch
observes us understandingly.

(*Collected Poems*, pp. 799ff)

Perfect Joy

Here is how I sum it up:

> Heaven does nothing: its non-doing is its serenity.
> Earth does nothing: its non-doing is its rest.
> From the union of these two non-doings
> All actions proceed,
> All things are made,
> How vast, how invisible
> This coming-to-be!
>
> All things come from somewhere!
> How vast, how invisible
> No way to explain it!
> All beings in their perfection
> Are born of non-doing.
> Hence it is said:
> "Heaven and earth do nothing
> Yet there is nothing they do not do."
>
> Where is the man who can attain
> To this non-doing?

(*Collected Poems*, pp. 896f)

Final Integration

Merton found a new freedom once he was allowed to lay aside the duties of novice master and to take up the "eremitical" life full time. He was himself ambivalent as to what to call his new life. Sometimes, as we will see in the following excerpts, he did not hesitate to identify it as an eremitical life. Other times, he denied it was such. He was just a man living in a "cabin" in the woods. The day he officially took up full-time residence there, he called it "a life free from care." Certainly, not free from caring, for as we have already seen, his caring about the human family and all its sufferings grew and grew. But he was free from many of the cares of community life and cenobitic monastic life with its liturgy and rituals and community events.

The greater freedom to use his time as he would gave Merton the opportunity to expand his interests and enter more deeply into some of the wide interests he already had. This was true especially in the religious sphere (which should surprise no one, for he remains all the more a monk, a man of God) and in the domain of interreligious dialogue. His gift for letter writing gained new scope and depth especially in this domain and reveals Merton ever more to us, this man of searching and expansive spirit.

With the resignation of Abbot James Fox and the election of Merton's own disciple, Flavian Burns, as abbot of Gethsemani, Merton also gained a new freedom to travel and to enter into face-to-face dialogue with some of the many with whom he had long corresponded. And he was able to explore far away places as possible new sites for a more secluded eremitical life. (When the new abbot stipulated it should be in the United States, Merton immediately opted to begin exploring Alaska. He also planned an exploration in Hawaii. How much further can you get from Gethsemani and still be in the United States?)

Yet as his interests and contacts ever expanded and he undertook far-flung travel and began to enjoy again some of the things of this world, Merton's spirit did not become dispersed. This may surprise some. Even some of his fellow Cistercians found it hard to understand how it all fit together in this monk's life. Yet those who have progressed far enough along the same path, who have with a certain constancy entered more and more deeply into the depths of their own center and passed through that center into the center of God, are not at all surprised. Everything is together in God.

In some ways Merton's last days on the Indian subcontinent characterize this. At the beginning of the week he is flying into Madras, very much the traditional Catholic pilgrim. Nine relics of saints in his pocket, he strains to see Mount Saint Thomas, the traditional site of the martyrdom of his patron, Saint Thomas the Apostle. He hastens to the cathedral to pray at the Apostle's tomb. He devoutly offers Mass on the Mount. Five days later he is walking bare-foot (much to the disgust of the eminent prelate who brought him there) at the great Buddhist shrine at Polonnaruwa and has one of the great "aesthetic illuminations" of his life. In between he stays at the finest hotel in Colombo, enjoys his scotch on the rocks and looks around for the best jazz band in town. It all fits together for him. "All problems are resolved and everything is clear, simply because what matters is clear . . . all matter, all life is charged . . . everything is emptiness and everything is compassion." Nothing more needs to be said.

"Even this is one sermon too many!"

The Monastic Life Is a Charismatic Vocation

The root question is the question of the authenticity of our monastic vocation. I mean this in a concrete sense again. I am not talking about the abstract value of our vocation. I am wondering if in fact we come to the monastery and *lose our monastic vocation when we have got there*. I mean, is it somehow squeezed out of us, so that we are left with the husk of outward forms and no inner vocation? Does our monastic life become so artificial and contrived that it is no longer really a life; it is just an existence which we put up with, a set of obligations which we fulfill, having as good intentions as we can muster, meanwhile looking for living interests elsewhere?

That is the trouble with the great overemphasis on monastic institutionalism. In fact, the monk comes to be for the sake of the monastery, not vice versa. The monk is a member of an organization. He cannot be fired, but he can be urged to work hard for the purposes of the organization, whatever they may be: from cheesemaking to liturgical renewal and "contemplation." In order to ensure that the monk will be more or less cooperative, he is told from morning to night that the monastic life consists purely and simply in doing what you are told. Sanctity, doing what you are told. Just do it, and keep your mouth shut, and that is all that is required. That is *everything*. It substitutes for prayer, for the spirit of prayer, for the desire of God (I use that bad word "desire"), it substitutes for meaningful activity. It substitutes for life itself.

This is not to say that obedience is not the "heart of monastic ascesis." It is. But merely doing what you're told is not obedience. And in order to make it obedience, a "pure intention" is not sufficient either. This unfortunate oversimplification of the monastic life is what drains it of all meaning and spirit. Then, after years of going to choir because one has been told that "this is the most sublime form of prayer you could possibly imagine, just because you have been told to do it," one suddenly wakes up and finds that the official convictions themselves have vanished. Then what? Everything is drained away. There is no interest left. The whole thing is meaningless.

This is a very dangerous situation, because at the moment I get the feeling that everyone is, as you say, more or less articulately admitting that they haven't been making any sense out of the office and have only been there fulfilling a duty. But to make this admission all right, acceptable, they are running around concocting new forms of the same thing. If the old office did not mean anything to them, where is the guarantee that the new one will mean more?

Merely singing the psalms in English is not going to make the office any deeper and any better for people who are just not interested in praying . . . when the office becomes too self-conscious and formal, when one has the feeling that it is what justifies the existence of the monastic community, something *for which* the monks exist, then I am not at home in it. But I realize that this is a perfectly legitimate view; it is the tradition of Cluny, and I admire it without wanting to live in it for myself. . . .

But your basic principles on *fuga mundi* [flight form the world], eschatological witness, and asceticism seem to me to be the real framework of the monastic life — more than that, its very being insofar as it is a search for God.

It seems to me that the monastic life is a charismatic vocation to fly from the world and seek the Gifts of the Spirit. We need the Holy Spirit because without Him we cannot pray, cannot resist the devil, cannot have real peace, cannot give witness to Christ and cannot live together as a community, still less as solitaries. The Holy Spirit is given to us, in choir, in the chanting of our psalms and our responses to the reading of the Word, and that is the reason for the office. Naturally one needs to understand what is happening and open one's heart to the Spirit.

When I say then that the problem is really one of authentic vocations, I think it comes to be in the end a question of whether of not we are extinguishing the Spirit by over-whelming the small sound of His voice by too much human clatter. I think the great problem of our monastic life, espe-cially when it gets big and unwieldy, is the ungodly prolifera-tion of human laws and regulations and systems and methods and projects and ideas. I don't care what the projects may be, how good the ideas may be in themselves, as long as they are chiefly the expedients and eccentricities of mere men looking for ways to assuage their anxieties and make themselves "happy," they will never do any good to anyone and they will not make monks of anyone. And if in order to promote all this waste of motion one is perpetually told to just "do what they say" and forget about the real reason why one came to the monastery, then the Spirit is extinguished.

I know this is not well explained and is dangerous talk anyway (everyone knows that the Holy Spirit is a dangerous illuminist). But bad though my expression of it may be, I think it comes somewhere near the truth.

This does not alter the fact that we must make changes, for they are precisely demanded of us by the Holy Spirit in the Church. But we must remember why we are making them and for whom.

(Letter to Father Ronald Roloff
The School of Charity, pp. 201–203)

The Right to Forget About Being Myself

In an age where there is much talk about "being yourself" I reserve to myself the right to forget about being myself, since in any case there is very little chance of my being anybody else. Rather it seems to me that when one is too intent on "being himself" he runs the risk of impersonating a shadow.

Yet I cannot pride myself on special freedom, simply because I am living in the woods. I am accused of living in the woods like Thoreau instead of living in the desert like St. John the Baptist. All I can answer is that I am not living "like anybody." Or "unlike anybody." We all live somehow or other, and that's that. It is a compelling necessity for me to be free to embrace the necessity of my own nature.

I exist under trees. I walk in the woods out of necessity. I am both a prisoner and an escaped prisoner. I cannot tell you why, born in France, my journey ended here in Kentucky. I have considered going further, but it is not practical. It makes no difference. Do I have a "day"? Do I spend my "day" in a "place"? I know there are trees here. I know there are birds here. I know the birds in fact very well, for there are precise pairs of birds (two each of fifteen or twenty species) living in the immediate area of my cabin. I share this particular place with them: for we form an ecological balance. This harmony gives the idea of "place" a new configuration.

As to the crows, they form part of a different pattern. They are vociferous and self-justifying, like humans. They are not two, they are many. They fight each other and the other birds, in a constant state of war.

There is a mental ecology, too, a living balance of spirits in this corner of the woods. There is room here for many other songs besides those of birds. Of Vallejo, for instance. Or Rilke, or Rene Char, Montale, Zukofsky, Ungaretti, Edwin Muir, Quasimodo or some Greeks. Or the dry, disconcerting voice of

Nicanor Parra, the poet of the sneeze. Here also is Chuang Tzu whose climate is perhaps most the climate of this scient corner of woods. A climate in which there is no need for explanation. Here is the reassuring companionship of many silent Tsu's and Fu's: Kung Tzu, Lao Tzu, Meng Tzu, Tu Fu. And Hui Neng. And Chao-Chu. And the drawings of Sengai. And a big graceful scroll from Suzuki. Here also is a Syrian hermit called Philoxenus. An Algerian cenobite called Camus. Here is heard the clanging prose of Tertullian, with the dry catarrh of Sartre. Here the voluble dissonances of Auden, with the golden sounds of John of Salisbury. Here is the deep vegetation of that more ancient forest in which the angry birds, Isaias and Jeremias, sing. Here should be, and are, feminine voices from Angela of Foligno to Flannery O'Connor, Teresa of Avila, Juliana of Norwich, and, more personally and warmly still, Raissa Maritain. It is good to choose the voices that will be heard in these woods, but they also choose themselves, send themselves here to be present in this silence. In any case, there is no lack of voices.

(*Day of a Stranger*, pp. 31–37)

The Real Thing about Being a Hermit

The real thing about being a hermit is of course that a hermit is outside all categories whatever. The hermit who succeeds, or thinks he can succeed, in simply having a recognizable niche — a nest of his own that everyone can account for and understand — may well be lacking an essential element of solitude. The hermit life is a kind of walking on water, in which one no longer can account for anything but one knows that one has not drowned and that this is to nobody's credit but God's. . . .

I agree that solitude is a really essential element in the religious life. One does have to cut loose and float away without ties, in one way or other, and those who try to get away from that aspect of it today are deceiving themselves. Perhaps there could be a less stark, less inhuman kind of loneliness in some communities, however . . .

My chief complaint about the hermit life is that a twenty-four hour day is not long enough to do what one would like to do. Really, didn't you find it slowed you down? I find I simply do not have the power to go on doing many things. I have to stop and vegetate. Eventually I may take root and turn into a plant. Certainly I am going to do much less work. I mean of the "productive" kind, publishable work. But I never know what kind of plan is going to come out. Everything is just what you don't expect.

(Letter to Father Aelred Squire
The School of Charity, p. 349)

My Daily Life in the Hermitage

. . . The main thing I can tell you without difficulty is the outline of my daily life in the hermitage.

The hermitage is ten minutes' walk from the monastery in a hidden place in the woods. No one comes there so the solitude is very good and appropriate for prayer, especially at night.

I go to bed about 7:30 at night and rise about 2:30 in the morning. On rising I say part of the canonical Office consisting of psalms, lessons, etc. Then I take an hour or an hour and a quarter for meditation. I follow this with some Bible reading and then make some tea or coffee and have breakfast if it is not a fast day. Breakfast consists of bread and tea or coffee, with perhaps a piece of fruit or some honey. With breakfast I begin reading and continue reading and studying until sunrise. Now the sun rises very late, in summer it rises earlier, so this period of study varies but it is on the average about two hours.

At sunrise I say another Office of psalms, etc., then begin my manual work, which includes sweeping, cleaning, cutting wood, and other necessary jobs. This finishes about nine o'clock, at which time I say another Office of psalms. If I have time then I may write a few letters, usually short (today is Sunday and I have more time). After this I go down to the monastery to say Mass, as I am not yet permitted to offer Mass in the hermitage. Saying Mass requires an altar, an acolyte who serves the Mass, special vestments, candles and so on. It is in a way better to have all this in the monastery. It would be hard to care for so many things and keep them clean in the hermitage. After Mass I take one cooked meal in the monastery. Then I return immediately to the hermitage usually without seeing or speaking to anyone except the ones I happen to meet as I go from place to place (these I do not ordinarily speak to as we have a rule of strict silence). (When I speak it is to the Abbot, whom I see once a week, or to someone in a position of authority, about necessary business.)

On returning to the hermitage I do some light reading, and then say another Office about one o'clock. This is followed by another hour or more of meditation. On feast days I can take an hour and a half or two hours for this afternoon meditation. Then I work at my writing. Usually I do not have more than an hour and a half or two hours at most for this, each day. Following that, it being now late afternoon (about four) I say another Office of psalms, and prepare for myself a light supper. I keep down to a minimum of cooking, usually only tea and soup, and make a sandwich of some sort. Thus I have

only a minimum of dishes to wash. After supper I have
another hour or more of meditation, after which I go to bed.

(Letter to Ch. Abdul Aziz
The Hidden Ground of Love, pp. 62–63)

Praise Rising Up
Out of the Center of Nothingness and Silence

Now you ask about my method of meditation. Strictly
speaking I have a very simple way of prayer. It is centered
entirely on attention to the presence of God and to His will
and His love. That is to say that it is centered on *faith* by which
alone we can know the presence of God. One might say this
gives my meditation the character described by the Prophet as
"being before God as if you saw Him." Yet it does not mean
imagining anything or conceiving a precise image of God, for
to my mind this would be a kind of idolatry. On the contrary, it
is a matter of adoring Him as invisible and infinitely beyond
our comprehension, and realizing Him as all. My prayer tends
very much toward what you call *fana*. There is in my heart this
great thirst to recognize totally the nothingness of all that is
not God. My prayer is then a kind of praise rising up out of
the center of Nothingness and Silence. If I am still present
"myself" this I recognize as an obstacle about which I can do
nothing unless He Himself removes the obstacle. If He wills
He can then make the Nothingness into a total clarity. If He
does not will, then the Nothingness seems to itself to be an
object and remains an obstacle. Such is my ordinary way of
prayer, or meditation. It is not "thinking about" anything, but
a direct seeking of the Face of the Invisible. I do not ordinarily
write about such things and I ask you therefore to be discreet
about it, but I write this as a testimony of confidence and

friendship. It will show you how much I appreciate the tradition of Sufism.

(Letter to Ch. Abdul Aziz
Hidden Ground of Love, pp. 63–64)

I am Tremendously Impressed with Sufism

I am tremendously impressed with the solidity and intellectual sureness of Sufism. There is no question but that here is a living and convincing truth, a deep mystical experience of the mystery of God our Creator Who watches over us at every moment with infinite love and mercy. I am stirred to the depths of my heart by the intensity of Moslem piety toward His Names, and the reverence with which He is invoked as the "Compassionate and the Merciful." May He be praised and adored everywhere forever.

It is because of this spirit of adoration and holy awe which is at the root of Sufism that the tree can reach such great heights and bear such bountiful fruits of love. . . . I want to say how much I like your article on Islam as vision and wisdom. The concept of wisdom as "Din" is very close to our monastic view of life, in which the wholeness of life itself, lived in prayer and in the understanding that is conferred by symbols, liturgy and contemplation, is a living wisdom and a constant communion with God the Source of all Wisdom. . . .

One of the chapters I like best . . . is that on the renewal of creation at each moment, and also that on the dhikr which resembles the techniques of the Greek monks, and I am familiar with its use, for it brings one close to God. . . .

Let us in any case have great love for Truth and open hearts to the Spirit of God our Lord and Father, Compassionate and Merciful. He alone is Real, and we have our reality only as a gift from Him at every moment. And at every moment it is our joy to be realized by Him over an abyss of nothingness: but the world has turned to the abyss and away from Him Who Is. That is why we live in dreadful times, and we must be brothers in prayer and worship no matter what may be the doctrinal differences that separate our minds.

(Letter to Ch. Abdul Aziz
Hidden Ground of Love, pp. 48–49)

Hasidism Itself is About Genuine Worldly Mysticism

I'd like to start today with this good little book of Martin Buber's. It's called *The Way of Man According to the Teaching of Hasidism*, a collection of tales about Hasidic rabbis who are very holy. Everyone should know about them because they reveal a biblical kind of mysticism. These stories also give us the right kind of this-worldliness, as opposed to the wrong kind we all know. Hasidism itself is about genuine worldly mysticism. This means it contains the awareness that all things are God's good creation. God has, so to speak, put something of the divine goodness in everything. There are holy sparks in all created beings. The human task is to see these things and to liberate the divine sparks in creation by praise, love, and joy.

In this view, all creation is waiting for us to come along and liberate the divine element in it, so that everything becomes one great blaze of glory to God. . . .

Buber tells a story about a rabbi who wanted to fast. The man was going to fast from Sabbath to Sabbath without any food or drink. He makes it till Thursday evening, when he gets very thirsty. He can't bear it any longer, so he goes to the well. But just as he gets there, he overcomes himself; he doesn't drink. Then he feels proud about this and thinks it would probably be better to overcome his pride and take a drink. When he goes to the well to overcome his pride, his thirst suddenly disappears. So he makes it until Saturday, having had this swing back and forth. Then he goes to report to the master, who takes one look at him and, before he can say anything, says, "Patchwork!"

Martin Buber then gives us a little meditation on this. He tells us that when he first heard the story he thought it was unfair. After all, the man did the job. He had to struggle and nearly lost, but he did succeed. Buber admits, however, that after a while he understood there was something wrong. Buber sees, and it's useful for us to see, that patchwork is the fruit of asceticism. If we try to do things ascetically, we may do them, but it usually ends up as patchwork. What we tend to do is to take the ascetic approach to everything — that is, we tend to think in terms of the will and self-conquest. If the emphasis is on self-conquest, we get patchwork.

This ties in with some notions on prayer. If prayer is something that we *do*, it's going to be patchwork, because I am a divided person, a divided being. So, in asceticism, I'm divided. Self-conquest is something I'm going to do; I've made up my mind to conquer myself. Then I must fight myself. I'm divided.

You may say, "Well, we're all divided. We just have to do this." But Buber says that actually what we need to do is first of all see that asceticism is completely secondary, and that asceticism isn't going to do the trick at all unless we are also supported by grace. The grace we need is the grace of unification. We have to wait until we sense that we're all of a piece before we try to do things like fasting for a whole week. One of the great things in the spiritual life and in monastic life is helping people realize when they've got everything together and are able to move.

This recognition is much more important than ascetic self-discipline by itself. People need to have a *taste* for fasting and things of that kind. We might ask, How are these people in the peace movement able to fast so much more than monks and nuns? They can go for three or four days with nothing. One thing, of course, is that they don't have a steady routine of being cut down to a rather low level of food the way we are. They can eat well most of the time, go out and get a good steak, so this means their bodies are better prepared for fasting.

But another very important factor is, these young people go into these things with a great deal of conviction. For example, if they are fasting on the steps of the Pentagon, they have somehow got themselves unified before they arrive there. They support one another; there's a kind of community spirit and almost a charismatic feeling that gets into them. This is good. We have lost that spirit because of the emphasis on asceticism, and a strong emphasis on individual asceticism. Each of us is left alone, more or less, to battle with ourselves and to wonder if we're not on trial in the eyes of others. If you get hungry and go for a piece of bread, you get worried that someone might see you. We've had some funny cases like that here, people who become obsessed with fear that they're going to collapse from hunger. So they store away a little snack. It doesn't have to be physical food, it might be a bunch of magazines. But something stored away, just in case. It's a bit silly, but it happens because people are not unified. It's important to be somehow together, of a piece, and united with others if we're going to fast.

It's the same thing in prayer. If I pray just because I think I ought to, or because I heard that it's a good thing to do, it's going to be patchwork. Then, when I ask how to pray, it's not going to help. I make a stab at it, I try a little Zen, it's going to be a mess. It will not really affect my life at all. This playing around with Zen is happening a lot. People hear about it, sit a little, pick up a few phrases, and feel better. But this does not unify their lives, and that's the purpose of Zen. It's supposed to get you so completely in one piece that it actually doesn't matter what you're doing. It's exactly the opposite of what people think. I mean, people think Zen stresses getting away from everything and sitting in constant recollection. That may be useful, it's the ascetic side of it, the patchwork. But actually, Zen makes you see that you *don't* have to do that, it helps you to be unified so that whether you're praying or working or whatever you're doing, it doesn't make much difference. You don't have to care. You don't have to make this or that distinction. Zen is fundamentally against this dividing, it *overcomes* division.

(*The Springs of Contemplation*, pp. 199–203)

The Heart of Catholicism, too, is a Living Experience

Buddhist meditation, but above all that of Zen, seeks not to *explain* but to *pay attention*, to *be mindful*, in other words to develop a certain *kind of consciousness that is above and beyond deception* by verbal formulas — or by emotional excitement. Deception in what? Deception in the grasp of itself as it really is. Deception due to diversion and distraction from what is right there — consciousness itself.

Zen, then aims at a kind of certainty: but it is not the logical certainty of philosophical proof, still less the religious certainty that comes with the acceptance of the word of God by the obedience of faith. It is rather the certainty that goes with an authentic metaphysical intuition which is also existential and empirical. The purpose of all Buddhism is to refine the consciousness until this kind of insight is attained and the religious implications of the insight are then variously worked out and applied to life in the different Buddhist traditions. . . .

It cannot be repeated too often in understanding Buddhism that it would be a great mistake to concentrate on the "doctrine," the formulated philosophy of life, and to neglect the experience, which is absolutely essential, the very heart of Buddhism. This is in a sense the exact opposite of the situation in Christianity. For Christianity begins with revelation. Though it would be misleading to classify this revelation simply as a "doctrine" and an "explanation" (it is far more than that — the revelation of God himself in the mystery of Christ) it is nevertheless communicated to us in words, in statements, and everything depends on the believer's accepting the truth of these statements.

Therefore Christianity has always been profoundly concerned with these statements; with the accuracy of their transmission from the original sources, with the precise understanding of their exact meaning, with the elimination and indeed the condemnation of false interpretations. At times this concern has been exaggerated almost to the point of an obsession, accompanied by arbitrary and fanatical insistence on hairsplitting distinction and the purest niceties of theological detail.

This obsession with doctrinal formulas, juridical order and ritual exactitude has often made people forget that the heart of Catholicism, too, is a *living experience* of unity in Christ which far transcends all conceptual formulations. What too often has been overlooked, in consequence, is that Catholicism is the taste and experience of eternal life: "We announce to you the eternal life which was with the Father and has appeared to us. What we have seen and have heard we announce to you, in order that you also may have fellowship with us and that our fellowship may be with the Father and with his Son Jesus Christ." (1 John 1.2–3) Too often the Catholic has imagined himself obliged to stop short at a mere correct and external belief expressed in good moral behavior instead of entering fully into the life of hope and love consummated by union with the invisible God "in Christ and in the Spirit," thus fully sharing in the Divine Nature. (Eph. 81.2 Pet. 1.4, Col. 1.9–17, 1 John 4.12–21).

The Second Vatican Council has (we hope) happily put an end to this obsessive tendency in Catholic theological investigation. But the fact remains that for Christianity, a religion of the Word, the understanding of the statements which embody God's revelation of himself remains a primary concern. Christian experience is a fruit of this understanding, a development of it, a deepening of it.

At the same time, Christian experience itself will be profoundly affected by the idea of revelation that the Christian himself will entertain. For example, if revelation is regarded simply as a system of truths *about* God and an explanation of how the universe came into existence, what will eventually happen to it, what is the purpose of Christian life, what are its moral norms, what will be the rewards of the virtuous, and so on, then Christianity is in effect reduced to a world view, at times a religious philosophy and little more, sustained by a more or less elaborate cult, by a moral discipline and a strict code of Law. "Experience" of the inner meaning of Christian revelation will necessarily be distorted and diminished in such a theological setting. What will such experience be? Not so much a living theological experience of the presence of God in the world and in mankind through the mystery of Christ, but rather a sense of security in one's own correctness; a feeling of confidence that one has been saved, a confidence which is based on the reflex awareness that one holds the correct view of the creation and purpose of the world and that one's behavior is of a kind to be rewarded in the next life. Or, perhaps, since few can attain this level of self-assurance, then the Christian experience becomes one of anxious hope — a struggle with occasional doubt of the "right answers," a painful and constant effort to meet the severe demands of morality and law, and a somewhat desperate recourse to the sacraments which are there to help the weak who must constantly fall and rise again.

This of course is a sadly deficient account of true Christian experience, based on a distortion of the true import of Christian revelation. Yet it is the impression non-Christians often get of Christianity from the outside.

(*Thomas Merton on Zen*, pp. 95–99)

Significant Clues

When we set Christianity and Buddhism side by side, we must try to find the points where a genuinely common ground between the two exists. At the present moment, this is no easy task. In fact it is still practically impossible . . . to really find any such common ground except in a very schematic and artificial way. After all, what do we mean by Christianity, and what do we mean by Buddhism? Is Christianity Christian theology? Ethics? Mysticism? Worship? Is our idea of Christianity to be taken without further qualifications as the Roman Catholic Church? Or does it include Protestant Christianity? The Protestantism of Luther or that of Bonhoeffer? The Protestantism of the God-is-dead school? The Catholicism of St. Thomas? Of St. Augustine and the Western Church Fathers? A supposedly "pure" Christianity of the Gospels? A demythologized Christianity ? A "social Gospel"? And what do we mean by Buddhism? The Theravada Buddhism of Ceylon, or that of Burma? Tibetan Buddhism? Tantric Buddhism? Pure Land Buddhism? Speculative and scholastic Indian Buddhism of the middle ages? Or Zen?

The immense variety of forms taken by thought, experience, worship, moral practice, in both Buddhism and Christianity make all comparisons haphazard, and in the end when someone like the late Dr. Suzuki announced a study on *Mysticism: Christian and Buddhist*, it turned out to be, rather practically in fact, a comparison between Meister Eckhart and Zen. To narrow the field in this way is at least relevant, though to take Meister Eckhart as representative of Christian mysticism is hazardous. At the same time we must remark that Dr. Suzuki was much too convinced that Eckhart was unusual in his time, and that his statements must have shocked most of his contemporaries. Eckhart's condemnation was in fact due in some measure to rivalry between Dominicans and Franciscans, and his teaching, bold and in some points unable to avoid condemnation, was nevertheless based on St. Thomas to a great extent and belonged to a mystical tradition that was very much alive and was, in fact, the most vital religious force in the Catholicism of his time. Yet to identify Christianity with Eckhart would be completely misleading. That was not what Suzuki intended. . . . He was not comparing the *mystical theology* of Eckhart with the Buddhist philosophy of the Zen masters, but the *experience* of Eckhart, ontologically and psychologically, with the *experience* of the Zen Masters. This is a reasonable enterprise, offering some small hope of interesting and valid results.

But can one distill from religious or mystical experience certain pure elements which are common everywhere in all religions? Or is the basic understanding of the nature and meaning of experience so determined by the variety of doctrines that a comparison of experiences involves us inevitably in a comparison of metaphysical or religious beliefs? This is no easy question either. If a Christian mystic has an experience which can be phenomenologically compared with a Zen experience, does it matter that the Christian in fact believes he is personally united with God and the Zen-man interprets his experience as *Sunyata* of the Void being aware of itself? In what sense can these two experiences be called "mystical"? Suppose that the Zen Masters forcefully repudiate any attempt on the part of Christians to grace them with the title of "mystics"?

It must certainly be said that a certain type of concordist thought today too easily assumes as a basic dogma that "the mystics" in all religions are all experiencing the same thing and are all alike in their liberation from the various doctrines and explanations and creeds of their less fortunate co-religionists. All religions thus "meet at the top," and their various theologies and philosophies become irrelevant when we see that they were merely means for arriving at the same end, and all means are alike efficacious. This has never been demonstrated with any kind of rigor, and though it has been persuasively advanced by talented and experienced minds, we must say that a great deal of study and investigation must be done before much can be said on this very complex question which, once again, seems to imply a purely formalistic view of theological and philosophical doctrines, as if a fundamental belief were something that a mystic could throw off like a suit of clothes and as if his very experience itself were not in some sense modified by the fact that he held this belief.

At the same time, since the personal experience of the mystic remains inaccessible to us and can only be evaluated indirectly through texts and other testimonials — perhaps written and given by others — it is never easy to say with any security that what a Christian mystic and a Sufi and a Zen Master experience is really "the same thing." What does such a claim really mean? Can it be made at all, without implying (quite falsely) that these higher experiences are "experiences of something"? It therefore remains a very serious problem to distinguish in all these higher forms of religious and metaphysical consciousness what is "pure experience" and what is to some extent determined by language, symbol, or indeed by the "grace of a sacrament." We have hardly reached the point where we know enough about these different states of consciousness and about their metaphysical implications to compare them in accurate detail. But there are nevertheless certain analogies and correspondence which are evident even now, and which may perhaps point out the way to a better mutual understanding. Let us not rashly take them as "proofs" but only as significant clues. . . .

The best we can say is that in certain religions, Buddhism for instance, the philosophical or religious framework is of a kind that *can* more easily be discarded, because it has in itself a built-in "ejector," so to speak, by which the mediator is at a certain point flung out from the conceptual apparatus into the Void. It is possible for a Zen Master to say nonchalantly to his disciple, "If you meet the Buddha, kill him!" But in Christian mysticism the question whether or not the mystic can get along without the human "form" (*Gestalt*) or the sacred Humanity of Christ is still hotly debated, with the majority opinion definitely maintaining the necessity for the Christ of faith to be present as an icon at the center of Christian contemplation. Here again, the question is confused by the failure to distinguish between the objective theology of Christian experience and the actual psychological facts of Christian mysticism in certain cases. And then one must ask, at what point do the abstract demands of theory take precedence over the psychological facts of experience? Or, to what extent does the theology of a theologian without experience claim to interpret correctly the "experienced theology" of the mystic who is perhaps not able to articulate the meaning of his experience in a satisfactory way?

(*Thomas Merton on Zen*, pp. 99–103)

Nothing . . . Except the Fact

Many of the Zen stories, which are almost always incomprehensible in rational terms, are simply the ringing of an alarm clock, and the reaction of the sleeper. Usually the misguided sleeper makes a response which in effect turns off the alarm so that he can go back to sleep. Sometimes he jumps out of bed with a shout of astonishment that it is so late. Sometimes he just sleeps and does not hear the alarm at all!

Insofar as the disciple takes the fact to be a sign of something else, he is misled by it. The Master may (by means of some other fact) try to make him aware of this. Often it is precisely at the point where the disciple realizes himself to be utterly misled that he also realizes everything else along with it: chiefly, of course, that there was nothing to realize in the first place except the fact. What *fact*? If you know the answer you are awake. You hear the alarm!

But we in the West, living in a tradition of stubborn ego-centered practicality and geared entirely for the use and manipulation of everything, always pass from one thing to another, from cause to effect, from the first to the next and to the last and then back to the first. Everything always points to something else, and hence we never stop anywhere because we cannot: as soon as we pause, the escalator reaches the end of the ride and we have to get off and find another one. Nothing is allowed just to be and to mean itself: everything has to mysteriously signify something else. Zen is especially designed to frustrate the mind that thinks in such terms. The Zen "fact," whatever it may be, always lands across our road like a fallen tree beyond which we cannot pass.

Nor are such facts lacking in Christianity — the Cross for example. Just as the Buddha's "Fire Storm" radically transforms the Buddhist's awareness of all that is around him, so the "word of the Cross" in very much the same way gives the

Christian a radically new consciousness of the meaning of his life and of his relationship with other men and with the world around him.

In both cases, the "facts" are not merely impersonal and objective, but facts of personal experience. Both Buddhism and Christianity are alike in making use of ordinary everyday human existence as material for a radical transformation of consciousness. Since ordinary everyday human existence is full of confusion and suffering, then obviously one will make good use of both of these in order to transform one's awareness and one's understanding, and to go beyond both to attain "wisdom" in love. It would be a great error to suppose that Buddhism and Christianity merely offer various *explanations* of suffering, or worse, justifications and mystifications built on this ineluctable fact. On the contrary both show that suffering remains inexplicable most of all for the man who attempts to *explain it in order to evade it*, or who thinks explanation itself is an escape. Suffering is not a "problem" as if it were something we could stand outside and control. Suffering, as both Christianity and Buddhism see, each in its own way, is part of our very ego-identity and empirical existence, and the only thing to do about it is to plunge right into the middle of contradiction and confusion in order to be transformed by what Zen call the "Great Death" and Christianity calls "dying and rising with Christ."

(*Thomas Merton on Zen*, pp. 107–109)

That is Zen

Where there is carrion lying, meat-eating birds circle and descend. Life and death are two. The living attack the dead, to their own profit. The dead lose nothing by it. They gain too, by being disposed of. Or they seem to, if you must think in terms of gain and loss. Do you then approach the study of Zen with the idea that there is something to be gained by it? This question is not intended as an implicit accusation. But it is, nevertheless, a serious question. Where there is a lot of fuss about "spirituality," "enlightenment" or just "turning on"; it is often because there are buzzards hovering around a corpse. This hovering, this circling, this descending, this celebration of victory, are not what is meant by the Study of Zen — even though they may be a highly useful exercise in other contexts. And they enrich the birds of appetite.

Zen enriches no one. There is no body to be found. The birds may come and circle for a while in the place where it is thought to be. But they soon go elsewhere. When they are gone, the "nothing," the "no-body" that was there, suddenly appears. That is Zen. It was there all the time but the scavengers missed it, because it was not their kind of prey.

What exactly, is Zen?

If we read the laconic and sometimes rather violent stories of the Zen Masters, we find that this is a dangerously loaded question: dangerous above all because the Zen tradition absolutely refuses to tolerate any abstract or theoretical answers to it. In fact, it must be said at the outset that philosophically or dogmatically speaking, the question probably has no satisfactory answer. Zen simply does not lend itself to logical analysis. The word "Zen" comes from the Chinese *Ch'an*, which designates a certain type of meditation, yet Zen is not a "method of meditation" or a kind of spirituality. It is a "way" and an "experience," a "life," but the way is paradoxically "not a way." Zen is therefore not a religion, not a philosophy, not a system of thought, not a doctrine, not an ascesis. In calling it a kind of "natural mysticism," Father Dumoulin is bravely submitting to the demands of Western thought, which is avid, at any price, for essences. But I think he would not find too many Eastern minds who would fully agree with him on this point, even though he is, in fact, giving Zen the highest praise he feels a Christian theologian can accord it. The truth is, Zen does not even lay claim to be "mystical," and the most widely read authority on the subject, Daisetz Suzuki, has expended no little effort in trying to deny the fact that Zen is "mysticism." This, however, is perhaps more a matter of semantics than anything else.

The Zen insight cannot be communicated in any kind of doctrinal formula or even *in any precise phenomenological description*. This is probably what Suzuki means when he says it is "not mystical": that it does not present clear and definitely recognizable characteristics capable of being set down in words. True, the genuineness of the Zen illumination is certainly recognizable, but only by one who has attained the insight himself. And here of course we run into the first of the abominable pitfalls that meet anyone who tries to write of Zen. For to suggest that it is "an experience" which a "subject" is capable of "having" is to use terms that contradict all the implications of Zen.

Hence it is quite false to imagine that Zen is a sort of individualistic, subjective purity in which the monk seeks to rest and find spiritual refreshment by the discovery and enjoyment of his own interiority. It is not a subtle form of spiritual self-gratification, a repose in the depths of one's own inner silence. Nor is it by any means a simple withdrawal from the outer world of matter to an inner world of spirit. The first and most elementary fact about Zen is its abhorrence of this dualistic division between matter and spirit. Any criticism of Zen that presupposes such a division is, therefore, bound to go astray.

Like all forms of Buddhism, Zen seeks an "enlightenment" which results from the resolution of all subject-object relationships and oppositions in a pure void. But to call this void a mere negation is to re-establish the oppositions which are resolved in it. This explains the peculiar insistence of the Zen masters on "neither affirming nor denying." Hence it is impossible to attain *satori* (enlightenment) merely by quietistic inaction or the suppression of thought. Yet at the same time "enlightenment" is not an experience or activity of a thinking and self-conscious subject. Still less is it a vision of Buddha, or an experience of an "I-Thou" relationship with a Supreme Being considered as object of knowledge and perception. However, Zen does not deny the existence of a Supreme Being either. It neither affirms nor denies, it simply *is*. One might say that Zen is the ontological *awareness of pure being beyond subject and object*, an immediate grasp of being in its "suchness" and "thusness."

But the peculiarity of this awareness is that it is not reflexive, not self-conscious, not philosophical, not theological. It is in some sense entirely beyond the scope of psychological observations and metaphysical reflection. For want of a better term; we may call it "purely spiritual."

(*Thomas Merton on Zen*, pp. xi – 3)

The Christian Approach

This discovery of the inner self plays a familiar part in Christian mysticism. But there is a significant difference, which is clearly brought out by St. Augustine. In Zen there seems to be no effort to get beyond the inner self. In Christianity the inner self is simply a stepping stone to an awareness of God. Man is the image of God, and his inner self is a kind of mirror in which God not only sees Himself, but reveals Himself to the "mirror" in which He is reflected. Thus, through the dark, transparent mystery of our own inner being we can, as it were, see God "through a glass." All this is of course pure metaphor. It is a way of saying that our being somehow communicates directly with the Being of God, Who is "in us." If we enter into ourselves, find our true self, and then pass "beyond" the inner "I," we sail forth into the immense darkness in which we confront the "I AM" of the Almighty. The Zen writers might perhaps contend that they were interested exclusively in what is actually "given" in their experience, and that Christianity is superadding a theological interpretation and extrapolation on top of the experience itself. But here we come upon one of the distinctive features of Christian, Jewish and Islamic mysticisms. For us, there is an infinite metaphysical gulf between the being of God and the being of the soul, between the "I" of the Almighty and our own inner "I." Yet paradoxically our inmost "I" exists in God and God dwells in it. But it is nevertheless necessary to distinguish between the experience of one's own inmost being and the awareness that God has revealed Himself to us in and through our inner self. We must know that the mirror is distinct from the image reflected in it. The difference rests on theological *faith*.

Our awareness of our inner self can at least theoretically be the fruit of a purely natural and psychological purification. Our awareness of God is a supernatural participation in the light by which He reveals Himself interiorly as dwelling in our inmost self. Hence the Christian mystical experience is not only an awareness of the inner self, but also, by a supernatural intensification of faith, it is an experiential grasp of God as present within our inner self.

(*The Inner Experience*, pp. 11–12)

The Message of a So-Called Contemplative to a So-Called Man of the World

This morning I received your letter of August 14th and I realize I must answer it immediately in order to get the reply to you before the end of the month. This does not leave me time to plan and think, and hence I must write rapidly and spontaneously. I must also write directly and simply, saying precisely what I think, and not pretending to announce a magnificent message which is really not mine. I will say what I can. It is not much. I will leave the rest of you to frame a document of good theology and clearly inspiring hope which will be of help to modern man in his great trouble.

On the other hand I must begin by saying that I was acutely embarrassed by the Holy Father's [Pope Paul VI] request. It puts us all in a difficult position. We are not experts in anything. There are few real contemplatives in our monasteries. We know nothing whatever of spiritual aviation and it would be the first duty of honesty to admit that fact frankly, and to add that we do not speak the language of modern man. There is considerable danger that in our haste to comply with the Holy Father's generous request, based on an even more generous estimate of us, we may come out with one more solemn pronouncement which will end not by giving modern man hope but by driving him further into despair, simply by convincing him that we belong to an entirely different world, in which we have managed, by dint of strong will and dogged refusals, to remain in a past era. I plead with you: we must at all costs avoid this error and act of uncharity. We must, before all else, whatever else we do, speak to modern man as his brothers, as people who are in very much the same difficulties as he is, as people who suffer much of what he suffers, though we are immensely privileged to be exempt from so many, so very many, of his responsibilities and sufferings. And we must not arrogate to ourselves the right to talk down to modern man, to dictate to him from a position of supposed eminence, when perhaps he suspects that our cloister walls have not done anything except confirm us in unreality. I must say these things frankly. I have seen over a thousand young men of our time, or rather nearly two thousand, enter and leave this monastery, coming with a hunger for God and leaving in a state of confusion, disarray, in comprehending frustration and often bitterness: because they could not feel that our claims here could be real for them. The problem of the contemplative Order at present, in the presence of modern man, is a problem of great ambiguity. People look at us, recognize we are sincere, recognize that we have indeed found a certain peace, and see that there may after all be some worth to it: but can we convince them that this means anything *to them*? I mean, can we convince them professionally and collectively, as "the contemplatives" in our walled institution, that what our institutional life represents has any meaning for them? If I were absolutely confident in answering yes to this, then it would be simple to draft the message we are asked to draw up. But to me, at least, it is not that simple. And for that reason I am perhaps disqualified from participating in this at all. In fact, this preface is in part a plea to be left out, to be exempted from a task to which I do not in the least recognize myself equal. However, as I said before, I will attempt to say in my own words what I personally, as an individual, have to say and usually do say to my brother who is in the world and who more and more often comes to me with his wounds which turn out to be also my own. The Holy Father, he can be a good Samaritan, but myself and my brothers in the world we are just two men who have fallen among thieves and we do our best to get each other out of the ditch.

Hence what I write here I write only as a sinner to another sinner, and in no sense do I speak officially for "the monastic Order" with all its advantages and its prestige and its tradition.

Let us suppose the message of a so-called contemplative to a so-called man of the world to be something like this:

My dear brother, first of all, I apologize for addressing you when you have not addressed me and have not really asked for anything. And I apologize for being behind a high wall which you do not understand. This high wall is to you a problem, and perhaps it is also a problem to me, O my brother. Perhaps you ask me why I stay behind it out of obedience? Perhaps you are no longer satisfied with the reply that if I stay behind this wall I have quiet, recollection, tranquility of heart. Perhaps you ask me what right I have to all this peace and tranquility when some sociologists have estimated that within the lifetime of our younger generation a private room will become an unheard-of luxury. I do not have a satisfactory answer: it is true, as an Islamic proverb says, "The hen does not lay eggs in the marketplace." It is true that when I came to this monastery where I am, I came in revolt against the meaningless confusion of a life in which there was so much activity, so much movement, so much useless talk, so much superficial and needless stimulation, that I could not remember who I was. But the fact remains that my flight from the world is not a reproach to you who remain in the world, and I have no right to repudiate the world in a purely negative fashion, because if I do that my flight will have taken me not to truth and to God but to a private, though doubtless pious, illusion.

Can I tell you that I have found answers to the questions that torment the man of our time? I do not know if I have found answers. When I first became a monk, yes, I was more sure of "answers." But as I grow old in the monastic life and advance further into solitude, I become aware that I have only begun to seek the questions. And what are the questions? Can man make sense out of his existence? Can man honestly give his life meaning merely by adopting a certain set of explanations which pretend to tell him why the world began and where it will end, why there is evil and what is necessary for a good life? My brother, perhaps in my solitude I have become as it were an explorer for you, a searcher in realms which you are not able to visit — except perhaps in the company of your psychiatrist. I have been summoned to explore a desert area of man's heart in which explanations no longer suffice, and in which one learns that only experience counts. An arid, rocky, dark land of the soul, sometimes illuminated by strange fires which men fear and peopled by specters which men studiously avoid except in their nightmares. And in this area I have learned that one cannot truly know hope unless he has found out how like despair hope is. The language of Christianity has been so used and so misused that sometimes you distrust it: you do not know whether or not behind the word "Cross" there stands the experience of mercy and salvation, or only the threat of punishment. If my word means anything to you, I can say to you that I have experienced the Cross to mean mercy and not cruelty, truth and not deception, that the news of the truth and love of Jesus is indeed the true good news, but in our time it speaks out in strange places. And perhaps it speaks out in you more than it does in me, perhaps Christ is nearer to you than He is to me, this I say without shame or guilt because I have learned to rejoice that Jesus is in the world in people who know Him not, that He is at work in them when they think themselves as from Him, and it is my joy to tell you to hope though you think that for you of all men hope is impossible. Hope not because you think you can be good, but because God loves us irrespective of our merits and whatever is good in us comes from His love, not from our own doing. Hope because Jesus is with those who are poor and outcasts and perhaps despised even by those who should seek them and care for them more lovingly because they act in God's name. . . . No one on earth has reason to despair of Jesus because Jesus loves man, loves him in his sin, and we too must love man in his sin.

God is not a "problem" and we who live the contemplative life have learned by experience that one cannot know God as long as one seeks to solve "the problem of God." To seek to solve the problem of God is to seek to see one's own eyes. One cannot see his own eyes because they are that with which he sees and God is the light by which we see — by which we see not a clearly defined "object" called God, but everything else in the invisible One. God is then the Seer and the Seeing and the Seen. God seeks Himself in us, and the aridity and sorrow of our heart is the sorrow of God who is not known in us, who cannot find Himself in us because we do not dare to believe or trust the incredible truth that He could live in us, and live there out of choice, out of preference. But indeed we exist solely for this, to be the place He has chosen for His presence, His manifestation in the world, His epiphany. But we make all this dark and inglorious because we fail to believe it, we refuse to believe it. It is not that we hate God, rather that we hate ourselves, despair of ourselves: if we once began to recognize, humbly but truly, the real value of our own self, we would see that this value was the sign of God in our being, the signature of God upon our being. Fortunately, the love of our fellow man is given us as the way of realizing this. For the love of our brother, our sister, our beloved, our wife, our child, is there to see with the clarity of God Himself that we are good. It is the love of my lover, my brother, of my child that sees God in me, makes God credible to myself in me. And it is the love for my lover, my child, my brother that enables me to show God to him or her in himself or herself. Love is the epiphany of God in our poverty. The contemplative life is then the search for peace not in an abstract exclusion of all outside reality, not in a barren negative closing of the senses upon the world, but in the openness of love. It begins with the acceptance of my own self in my poverty and my nearness to despair in order to recognize that where God is there can be no despair, and God is in me even if I despair. That nothing can change God's love for me, since my very existence is the sign that God loves me and the presence of His love creates and sustains me. Nor is there any need to understand how this can be or to explain it or to solve the problems it seems to raise. For there is in our hearts and in the very ground of our being a natural certainty which is co-extensive with our very existence: a certainty that says that insofar as we exist we are penetrated through and through with the sense and reality of God even though we may be utterly unable to believe or experience this in philosophic or even religious terms.

O my brother, the contemplative is the man not who has fiery visions of the cherubim carrying God on their imagined chariot, but simply he who has risked his mind in the desert beyond language and beyond ideas where God is encountered in the nakedness of pure trust, that is to say in the surrender of our poverty and incompleteness in order no longer to clench our minds in a cramp upon themselves, as if thinking made us exist. The message of hope the contemplative offers you, then, brother, is not that you need to find your way through the jungle of language and problems that today surround God: but that whether you understand or not, God loves you, is present in you, lives in you, dwells in you, calls you, saves you, and offers you an understanding and light which are like nothing you ever found in books or heard in sermons. The contemplative has nothing to tell you except to reassure you and say that if you dare to penetrate your own silence and risk the sharing of that solitude with the lonely other who seeks God through you, then you will truly recover the light and the capacity to understand what is beyond words and beyond explanations because it is too close to be explained: it is the intimate union in the depths of your own heart, of God's spirit and your own secret inmost self, so that you and He are in all truth One Spirit, I love you in Christ.

(Letter to Dom Francis Decroix
The Hidden Ground of Love, pp. 154–158)

Maybe the End
is Much Closer than We Think

Today I came across an article about progress and regress in history. It says something new and I think it makes a good point. It starts with the idea of means and ends. In the normal succession of things that we deal with every day, the ends are implied in the means. For example, if you want to use a hammer, you don't sit down and put the hammer on the table and meditate on it. You pick it up and drive a nail into the wall. When you're driving the nail into the wall, you're not thinking about the hammer, you're thinking about getting the nail in the wall. Later on, you'll hammer another nail, and so on. One thing naturally leads to another. This is an "ordinary succession of things." This is the way things normally progress, which implies making use of the means that you have toward the ends that are built into the means.

Now, we all realize and have observed that, in our modern world, instead of having a means which leads to an end, you start something first. Then you invent an end to justify why you're doing it. A rich man starts a foundation because he wants his millions to be tax-exempt, then he finds a purpose for the foundation. This gets to be more and more of a pattern. Instead of having ends, you are reflecting back on the means all the time. This leads to the means becoming the end. So means become sort of autonomous, they work by themselves.

I think the relevance of this is clear. We're liable to do this very thing in religious change, to get distracted from the fact that we have real ends to attain and that there's a normal progression toward them. We can fall into one of those vicious circles where life just goes round and round without getting anywhere. We start doing something and then invent a reason to justify doing it. Think of the implications of this. The Vietnam war is in our minds all the time. And it strikes me that a lot of the wars we have are wars that somebody has started to prove that we ought to have a war, to prove that war is necessary. Or, as Simone Weil put it, you start a war and a thousand soldiers are killed. After that, you're committed. You have to go back and fight some more, because these thousand dead will haunt you if you don't go and avenge them. This is an illustration of original sin, the way it gets into the whole war picture.

This article develops the idea further and says that maybe the reason people stop going forward and start going back is that they're already near the end and they don't want to reach it. For example, world peace is now possible, it's in sight. With a bit more effort and a bit more sense, we could have it. Leaders may be backtracking into wars on all sides because we just don't know how to cope with peace.

This may be the way it is with us in our lives. Maybe the end is much closer than we think. Nobody can really stop us. There is such a thing as rebellion in order to justify submission. This is an adolescent trait. We see it in kids: a teenager who fights because he wants to be slapped down — he's never been slapped down before so he starts a fight to make it happen. Then he has a grievance for fighting some more and the cycle is repeated.

Sometimes, in our attitude toward authorities — who can be a nuisance, it's true — we can do this. But we don't have to get into that kind of a bind. Maybe the ends are much closer to us than we realize. . . .

Built into us is a kind of desire for the end, and yet a fear of it, too. We want to attain these things that are beyond us, but we're afraid. As you start getting closer to union with God, it gets tough and we're not really 100 percent for it anyway. So a great deal in us rebels. We've been through the death that's necessary for us to get this far. Now we want to see if we can't work out some kind of a deal so that we can really progress by staying where we are. This is the way we're built as human beings. So we're tempted just to spin all this out in intellectual terms and not really change at all.

But, of course, we're not allowed to do that for long. If we have just enough confidence to let God grab us by the scruff of the neck and drag us through the next thing when we least expect it, then we've got it, we're all right. And we help other people do that as far as we can. I feel very confident about this. None of us is being fooled, we've been through enough to know it's real, that what we are doing is on the level. We are going in the right direction.

(*The Springs of Contemplation*, pp. 111–119)

I am on the Pacific Shore

I am on the Pacific Shore — perhaps fifty miles south of Cape Mendocino. Wide open, deserted hillside frequented only by sheep and swallows, sun and wind. No people for miles either way. Breakers on the black sand. Crying gulls fly down and land neatly on their own shadows.

I am half way between Needle Rock where there is an abandoned house, and Bear Harbor, where there is another abandoned house — 3 miles between them. No human habitation in sight on all the miles of shore line either way, though there is a small sheep ranch hidden beyond Needle Rock.

North, toward Shelter Cove, a manufactory of clouds where the wind piles up smoky moisture along the steep flanks of the mountains. Their tops are completely hidden.

Back inland, in the Mattole Valley at the convent, it is probably raining.

South, bare twin pyramids. And down the shore, a point of rock on which there is a silent immobile convocation of seabirds, perhaps pelicans.

Far our at sea, a long low coastal vessel seems to get nowhere. It hangs in an isolated patch of light like something in eternity.

And yet, someone has been here before me with a small box of sun-kissed seedless raisins and I too have one of these. So this other may have been a nun from the Redwoods.

A huge shark lolls in the swells making his way southward, close in shore, showing his dorsal fin.

Faint cry of lamb on the mountain side muffled by sea wind.

When I came four or five days ago to Needle Rock, I told the rancher I would be out on this mountainside for a few days. He had just finished shearing. All the sheep were still penned in at the ranch. Now they are all over the mountain again.

This morning I sheltered under a low thick pine while sheep stood bare and mute in the pelting shower.

Song sparrows everywhere in the twisted trees — "Neither accept or reject anything." *Astavakra Gita*

Low tide. Long rollers trail white sleeves of foam behind them, reaching for the sand, like hands for the keyboard of an instrument. . . .

Not to run from one thought to the next, says Theophane the Recluse, but to give each one time to settle in the heart.

Attention. Concentration of the spirit in the heart.

Vigilance. Concentration of the will in the heart.

Sobriety. Concentration of feeling in the heart.

Bear Harbor is in many ways better than Needle Rock — more isolated, more sheltered. A newer house, in better repair, with a generator. You reach it finally after barns, and the tall eucalyptus grove.

Flowers at Bear Harbor. Besides wild irises three or four feet high, there are calla lilies growing wild among the ferns on the stream bank. A profusion of roses and a lot of flowering shrubs that I cannot name.

Bear Harbor — rocky cove piled up with driftwood logs, some of which have been half burned. Much of it could serve as firewood.

When Father Roger drove me out here this morning, it was low tide. Four cars or trucks were parked by the old dead tree at Needle Rock and people were fishing for abalone. Two other cars met us on the road as we went down. That's too many.

There were even two cars at Bear Harbor and two pairs of young men . . . one of them a teacher interested in Zen.

About a mile from Bear Harbor, there is a hollow in which I am now sitting where one could comfortably put a small trailer. A small loud stream, many quail.

The calm ocean . . . very blue through the trees. Calla lilies growing wild. A very active flycatcher. The sun shines through his wings as through a Japanese fan. It is the feast of St. Pachomius. Many ferns. A large unfamiliar hawk-type bird flew over a little while ago, perhaps a young eagle. . . .

"How many incarnations hast thou devoted to the actions of body, mind and speech? They have brought thee nothing but pain. Why not cease from them?" *Astavakra Gita*

Reincarnation or not, I am as tired of talking and writing as if I had done it for centuries. Now it is time to listen at length to this Asian ocean. Over there, Asia.

Yesterday, in this place, looking southwest, I thought of New Zealand and the *Wahine* and my Aunt Kit getting into the last lifeboat. It capsized.

I was sitting in the shade near the spot where the jay cried out on the branch over my head yesterday and awakened me as I was dozing in the sun. A red pick-up truck came up the dirt road. The owner of the land was in it with his wife and said he would be willing to rent me his house at Bear Harbor if plans work out for him in September but he can't commit himself until then.

(*Woods, Shore, Desert*, pp. 14–21)

Need to Push On to the Great Doubt

In our monasticism, we have been content to find our way to a kind of peace, a simple undisturbed thoughtful life. And this is certainly good, but is it good enough?

I for one, realize that now I need more. Not simply to be quiet, somewhat productive, to pray, to read, to cultivate leisure — *otium sanctum*! There is a need of effort, deepening, change and transformation. Not that I must undertake a special project of self-transformation or that I must "work on my self." In that regard, it would be better to forget it. Just to go for walks, live in peace, let change come quietly and invisibly on the inside.

But I do have a past to break with, an accumulation of inertia, waste, wrong, foolishness, rot, junk, a great need of clarification of mindfulness, or rather of no mind — a return to genuine practice, right effort, need to push on to the great doubt. Need of the Spirit.

Hang on to the clear light!

(*Woods, Shore, Desert*, p. 48)

My Plans Are

My plans are to spend just a day here [New Delhi]. . . . Monday I go to Calcutta on the way to Darjeeling (didn't get there for the meeting, floods and landslides prevented it); the meeting was in Calcutta and on the whole, looking back, it was pretty poor. But I made a couple of good friends. Incidentally a *Life* photographer was there, but I hope none of his stuff will be considered important enough to print — it wasn't.

I'll be in Darjeeling-Sikkim area for a couple of weeks, meeting mostly Tibetans, and also studying and praying in the mountains. It is near Mt. Everest (at least Everest is visible from there). Then I go to Madras in S. India where there is a shrine of St. Thomas, supposedly the site of his martyrdom. I'll remember you at Mass there. Then to Ceylon [Sri Lanka], for the Theravada Buddhists, then to the Bangkok meeting. I am not sure of the exact date of that meeting, and have no information, but hope there will be some in Calcutta. If you or Bro. Patrick know the date and where we are supposed to meet and live, please let me know, in case no other letter has reached me.

After the meeting, then Indonesia as planned and so on through to Japan. After Japan, I believe it is necessary to make a change of plans. I was going to fly back to San Francisco via Hawaii in April or so, but the Dalai Lama suggested that I speak to some people in Europe, including a Tibetan who is setting up a monastery in Switzerland, and also this Abbot friend of mine has a meditation center in Scotland. I ought also to see Marco Pallis who is one of the great experts on Tibetan Buddhism, and another expert in Wales. I can fly from Tokyo over the N. Pole to Europe and take in Switzerland and Scotland, avoiding Cistercian monasteries as much as possible and keeping out of sight, coming back to the U.S. about the end of May. Please let me know if this is ok with you, and I can plan accordingly.

I assume that when I get back to the U. S. you would want me to come back to Gethsemani and we could plan any further steps from there. I am still keen on the idea of trying something in Alaska and I am certain of full support from the bishop there. But naturally this would have to be planned carefully with you, and in the light of whatever may come up between then and now. I often think of the hermitage at Gethsemani and of the many graces it has meant to me: but I still think that I ought to be elsewhere, though always as a member of my monastic family there. I am certainly willing to go slow and be patient about it. But let's be thinking about it and praying to know God's will.

(Letter to Abbot Flavian Burns, Nov. 9, 1968
The School of Charity, pp. 410–411)

I Have Now Seen
and Have Pierced Through

The path dips down to Gal Vihara: a wide, quiet, hollow, surrounded with trees. A low outcrop of rock, with a cave cut into it, and beside the cave a big seated Buddha on the left, a reclining Buddha on the right, and Ananda, I guess, standing at the head of the reclining Buddha. . . . I am able to approach the Buddhas barefoot and undisturbed, my feet in wet grass, wet sand. Then the silence of the extraordinary faces. The great smiles. Huge and yet subtle. Filled with every possibility, questioning nothing, knowing everything, rejecting nothing, the peace not of emotional resignation but of Madhyamika, of sunyata, that has seen through every question without trying to discredit anyone or anything — *without refutation* — without establishing some argument. For the doctrinaire, the mind that needs well-established positions, such peace, such silence, can be frightening. I was knocked over with a rush of relief and thankfulness at the *obvious* clarity of the figures, the clarity and fluidity of shape and line, the design of the monumental bodies composed into the rock shape and landscape, figure, rock and tree. And the sweep of bare rock sloping away on the other side of the hollow, where you can go back and see different aspects of the figures.

Looking at these figures I was suddenly, almost forcibly jerked clean out of the habitual, half-tied vision of things, and an inner clearness, clarity, as if exploding from the rocks themselves, became evident and obvious. The queer *evidence* of the reclining figure, the smile, the sad smile of Ananda standing with arms folded. . . . The thing about all this is that there is no puzzle, no problem and really no "mystery." All problems are resolved and everything is clear, simply because what matters is clear. The rock, all matter, all life, is charged with *dharmakaya* . . . everything is emptiness and everything is compassion. I don't know when in my life I have ever had such a sense of beauty and spiritual validity running together in one aesthetic illumination. Surely, with Mahabalipuram and Polonnaruwa my Asia pilgrimage has come clear and purified itself. I mean, I know and I have seen what I was obscurely looking for. I don't know what else remains but I have now seen and have pierced through the surface and got beyond the shadow and the disguise.

(*The Asian Journal*, 233–235)

Cistercian Simplicity

Hence we see that the very essence of Cistercian simplicity is the practice of charity and loving obedience and mutual patience and forbearance in the community life which should be on earth an image of the simplicity of heaven. We begin to see something of the depth of this beautiful Cistercian ideal!

Cistercian simplicity, then begins in humility and self-distrust, and climbs through obedience to the perfection of fraternal charity to produce that unity and peace by which the Holy and Undivided Trinity is reflected not only in the individual soul but in the community, in the Order, in the Church of God. Once a certain degree of perfection in this social simplicity is arrived at on earth, God is pleased to bend down and raise up the individuals who most further this unity by their humility and love to a closer and far more intimate union with Him by mystical prayer, mystical union.

The culmination of Cistercian simplicity is the mystical marriage of the soul with God, which is nothing else but the perfect union of our will with God's will, made possible by the complete purification of all the duplicity of error and sin. This purification is the work of love and particularly of the love of God in our neighbor. Hence it is inseparable from that social simplicity which consists in living out the *voluntas communis* [the common will] in actual practice.

This, then, is the ultimate limit of Cistercian simplicity: the simplicity of God Himself, belonging to the soul, purified of all admixture of self-love, admitted to a participation in the Divine Nature, and becoming one Spirit with the God of infinite love.

(The Spirit of Simplicity, pp. 124–135)

For God is Love

There is only one reason for the monk's existence: not farming, not chanting the psalms, not building beautiful monasteries, not wearing a certain kind of costume, not fasting, not manual labor, not reading, not meditation, not vigils in the night, but only God.

And that means: love. For God is love. If we love him we possess him. Everything else about the monastic life is only a means to that end. When prayer and penance and all the rest cease to be means and become ends in themselves, the contemplative life stops dead and the monk begins to amble along the broad, dreary paths that are trodden by the multitudes of the world.

Therefore, there is a limit to the value of all the methods and means the monk uses to acquire the love of God. His external activities can be carried beyond what the economist would call a "point of diminishing returns." That holds for prayer as well as for penance, for fasting as well as for contemplation, for liturgy as well as for manual labor: all these things are valuable only up to a certain point. Beyond that limit they do harm instead of good. What is the limit? St. Bernard long ago explained to monks that the exterior acts prescribed by monastic rules were valuable only to the extent that they favored the growth of interior charity. It is no good to fast beyond the point where fasting and charity come in conflict, or to pray when it interferes with the love you owe to your brothers or to God.

But there is one thing in life that has no limit to its value, one virtue that can be practiced without any need for moderation. And that is *love;* the love of God and the love of other men in God and for his sake. *There is no point at which it becomes reasonable to abate your interior love for God or for other men, because that love is an end in itself: it is the thing for which we were created and the only reason why we exist.* Only the exterior acts which are means to this end have to be moderated, because otherwise they would not serve as means and would not bring us to the end. But when the end itself is reached, there is no limit, no need of saying, "It is enough."

In fact, if you discover any kind of love that satiates you, it is not the end for which you were created. Any act that can cease to be a joy is not the end of your existence. If you grow tired of a love that you thought was the love of God, be persuaded that what you are tired of was never pure love, but either some act ordered to that love or else something without order altogether.

The one love that always grows weary of its object and is never satiated with anything and is always looking for something different and new is the love of ourselves. It is the source of all boredom and all restlessness and all unquiet and all misery and all unhappiness; ultimately, it is hell.

(*The Waters of Siloe*, pp. 335–336)

Apothegmata

"The young man went to the Father and said: Father, give me a word of life." This was the customary way, which prevails even until today among more devout Byzantine Christians, in which one sought guidance on the spiritual path. In response the Father would give the disciple a "word" — a word, phrase or sentence — often drawn from Scripture, which the disciple would repeat in his mind and even on his lips until it formed his heart, "until the mind descended into the heart." It was not so much a question of thinking the thing over, getting it in some way to fit into the context of the thoughts one already has, but rather of letting the insight expand one's consciousness and open the heart to a new perception of Reality.

We offer here just a few of the many *apothegmata* that one could draw from the writings of Thomas Merton. Each has the possibility of altering our consciousness — for the better.

.

Nothing can change God's love for me, since my very existence is the sign that God loves me.

(*The Hidden Ground of Love*, p. 157)

Souls are like athletes, that need opponents worthy of them, if they are to be tried and extended and pushed to the full use of their powers, and rewarded according to their capacity.

(*Seven Storey Mountain*, p. 83)

How far I have to go to find you in whom I have already arrived!

(*Seven Storey Mountain*, p. 419)

Evil is not only reversible but it is the proper motive of that mercy by which it is overcome and changed into good.

(*Gandhi on Non-Violence*, p. 12)

Only the admission of defect and fallibility in oneself makes it possible for one to become merciful to others.

(*Gandhi on Non-Violence*, p. 12)

We put words between ourselves and things. Even God has become another conceptual unreality in a no man's land of language that no longer serves as a means of communion with reality.

(*Thoughts in Solitude*, p. 83)

We do not really know how to forgive until we know what it is to be forgiven.

(*Thoughts in Solitude*, p. 83)

If we are without human feelings we cannot love God in the way in which we are meant to love him — as men.

(*Thoughts in Solitude*, p. 83)

It is the love of my lover . . . that sees God in me, makes God credible to myself in me. And it is my love for my lover . . . that enables me to show God to him or her in himself or herself.

(*The Hidden Ground of Love*, p. 157)

Love is the epiphany of God in our poverty.

(*The Hidden Ground of Love*, p. 157)

We live as spiritual men when we live as men seeking God.

(*Thoughts in Solitude*, p. 83)

Life reveals itself to us only insofar as we live it.

(*Thoughts in Solitude*, p. 83)

We must see and accept the mystery of God's love in our own apparently inconsequential lives.

(*The New Man*, p. 231)

Stopping too soon is the commonest dead-end in prayer.

(*The Climate of Monastic Prayer*, p. 154)

Sermon to the birds: "Esteemed friends, birds of noble lineage, I have no message to you except this: be what you are: be *birds*. Thus you will be your own sermon to yourselves!"

Reply: "Even this is one sermon too many!"

(*Day of a Stranger*, p. 51)

"How do I know which is the better choice?"
If you are choosing for life, for a living entity, it's a better choice. If you're choosing for a dead, rigid thing, it's a worse choice. Even if a choice turns out to be imprudent, there's a built-in safeguard because it's *alive*, it's warm, it's real. We have to choose life always.

(*The Springs of Contemplation*, p. 126)

The deepest level of communication is not communication but communion. It is wordless. It is beyond words and it is beyond speech and it is beyond concepts.

(*The Asian Journal*, p. 308)

My dear brothers, we are already one. But we imagine that we are not. And what we have to recover is our original unity.

(*The Asian Journal*, p. 308)

What we have to be is what we are.

(*The Asian Journal*, p. 308)

Sources

It might help readers appreciate the passages selected for this volume and might also interest them to hear how Thomas Merton himself summed up his literary output less than six months before his early death. He did so in this letter to an anonymous sister.

The only things I wrote before my conversion were juvenile pieces published in college magazines. And maybe a book review or two. None of it counts for anything.

I'd rather divide as follows: from my conversion in 1938 to my ordination in 1949 — that is, up to *Seven Storey Mountain*, *Waters of Siloe*, etc., when I suddenly got to be well known, a best-seller, etc. Then a long period until somewhere in the early sixties, a transition period which would end somewhere around *Disputed Questions*. During the first period, after entering the monastery, I was totally isolated from all outside influences and was largely working with what I had accumulated before entering. [I drew] on the experience of the monastic life in my early days when I was quite ascetic, "first fervor" stuff, and when the life at Gethsemani was very strict. This resulted in a highly unworldly, ascetical, intransigent, somewhat apocalyptic outlook. Rigid, arbitrary separation between God and the world, etc. Most people judge me entirely by this period, either favorably or unfavorably, and do not realize that I have changed a great deal. The second period was a time when I began to open up again to the world, began reading psychoanalysis (Fromm, Horney, etc.), Zen Buddhism, existentialism and other things like that, also more literature. But the fruits of this did not really begin to appear until the third period, after *Disputed Questions*. This resulted in books like *Seeds of Destruction, Raids on the Unspeakable, Conjectures of a Guilty Bystander, Emblems of a Season of Fury, Chuang Tzu*, etc. It appears that I am now evolving further, with studies on Zen and a new kind of experimental creative drive in prose poetry, satire, etc.

> Characteristic books of the first period: *Secular Journal, Thirty Poems, Man in the Divided Sea, Seven Storey Mountain, Seeds of Contemplation*.
>
> Characteristic of second: *No Man Is an Island, Sign of Jonas, Thoughts in Solitude, Silent Life, Strange Islands*.
>
> Third period — I've mentioned them above I guess, and (I might add) important to some extent is the introduction to *Gandhi on Non-Violence*. I guess the essay on Pasternak in *Disputed Questions* might throw light on it. Also see Preface to *Thomas Merton Reader* and interview in *Motive* (reprint in *U. S. Catholic* for March [1968]).

Yes, I have a lot of critics, particularly among Catholics. These are usually people who have seen one aspect of my work which they don't like. Most of them are put off by the fact that I sound at times like a Catholic Norman Mailer. I get on better with non-Catholics, particularly the younger generation, students, hippies, etc. At the same time there is always a solid phalanx of people who seem to get a lot out of the early books up to about *Thoughts in Solitude*, and have never heard of the others. These tend to be people interested in the spiritual life and somewhat conservative in many ways. Hence the curious fact that there are by and large two Mertons: one ascetic, conservative, traditional, monastic. The other radical, independent, and somewhat akin to beats and hippies and to poets in general. Neither one of these appeals to the current pacesetters for Catholic thought and life in the U. S. today. Some of them respect me, others think I'm nuts, none of them really digs me. Which is perfectly all right. Where I fit seems to be in the sort of niche provided by the *Catholic Worker* — and outside that, well, the literary magazines whether little or otherwise. Mostly, little. And New Directions, [the publishing house] where I have always been.

I guess that's about it. Looking back on my work, I wish I had never bothered to write about one-third of it — the books that tend to be (one way or the other) "Popular" religion. Or "inspirational." But I'll stand by things like *Seeds of Contemplation* (as emended in *New Seeds*). *Seven Storey Mountain* is a sort of phenomenon, not all bad, not all good, and it's not something I could successfully repudiate even if I wanted to. Naturally I have reservations about it because I was young then and I've changed. . . .

(*The School of Charity*, pp. 384–385)

A Brief Chronology

1915   January 31: born in Prades, France

1916   Moves to the United States with parents

1921   October 3: his mother, Ruth Jenkins Merton, dies of cancer

1922   Goes to Bermuda with his father

1923   Returns to Douglaston, New York, to live with Ruth Merton's parents

1925   Moves to France with his father; they settle at St. Antonin

1926   Begins studies at Lycee Ingres, Montauban, France

1928   May: moves to England and continues his studies at Ripley Court

1929   Easter: at Canterbury with his father.
        August: goes to Aberdeen, Scotland, and his father enters the hospital in London.
        Fall: enters Oakham Public School in Rutland, England

1930   June: Grandfather Jenkins gives him financial in-
            dependence
            Christmas recess: goes to Strasbourg

1931   January 18: his father, Owen Merton, dies of a brain
            tumor
            Easter recess: goes to Florence and Rome
            Summer: visits the United States
            Fall: editor of the *Oakhamian*; writes on Gandhi

1932   Easter recess: visits Germany
            September: attains a higher certificate
            December: wins a scholarship to Clare College,
            Cambridge

1933   February: goes across France to Rome for a prolonged
            visit
            Summer: visits the United States
            Fall: begins classes at Cambridge

1934   Summer: visits the United States
            Fall: returns to England to obtain resident visa for the
            United States

1935   January: begins classes at Columbia University
            Spring: joins and leaves the Communist Party

1936   October 30: his grandfather, Samuel Jenkins, dies

1937   Editor of the Columbia *Yearbook*; art editor of the *Jester*.
            February: reads Etienne Gilson's *The Spirit of Medieval
            Philosophy*
            August 16: his grandmother, Martha Jenkins, dies

1938   Receives his Bachelor of Arts degree and begins to work
            for his Master of Arts
            August: Mass at Corpus Christi
            Fall: moves to 114th Street apartment; studies under
            Dan Walsh
            November 16: baptized as a Roman Catholic

1939   February 22: receives his Master of Arts degree
        Visits Bermuda, moves to Perry Street in the Village
        Teaches at Columbia University Extension and writes
        book reviews for New York newspapers
        May 29: receives the sacrament of Confirmation
        Summer: lives in Olean, New York, with Lax and Rice;
        writes *The Labyrinth*
        Fall: begins teaching English at St. Bonaventure's
        College
        November: applies to join the Franciscans

1940   April-May: visits Cuba
        June: rejected as an applicant by the Franciscans
        Summer: at Olean

1941   Easter: retreat at the Abbey of Gethsemani
        September: retreat at Our Lady of the Valley Trappist
        Abbey, Cumberland, Rhode Island
        December 10: enters the Abbey of Gethsemani

1942   February 21: receives the novices' habit and the
        monastic name of Frater Mary Louis

1944   March 19: temporary profession
        Thirty Poems

1946   *A Man in the Divided Sea*

1947   March 19: solemn profession, consecration as a monk

1948   August 4: death of Abbot Frederic Dunne
        August 23: election of Abbot James Fox
        December 21: ordained subdeacon.
        *Exile Ends in Glory, Figures of an Apocalypse, The Seven
        Storey Mountain, The Spirit of Simplicity, What Is
        Contemplation?*

1949   May 26: ordained a priest
        *The Tears of the Blind Lions, Seeds of Contemplation, The
        Waters of Siloe*

1950   *Selected Poems, What Are These Wounds?*

1951   May: master of students at Gethsemani
          The Ascent to Truth

1952   July: visit to Ohio
          Bread in the Wilderness, The Sign of Jonas

1954   *The Last of the Fathers*

1955   Master of novices
          No Man Is an Island

1956   *The Living Bread, Praying the Psalms, Silence in Heaven*

1957   *The Basic Principles of Monastic Spirituality, The Silent Life, The Strange Islands, The Tower of Babel*

1958   March 18: the enlightenment at Fourth and Walnut
          Monastic Peace, Nativity Kerygma, Thoughts in Solitude

1959   *The Secular Journal of Thomas Merton, Selected Poems of Thomas Merton*

1960   October: building the hermitage
          Disputed Questions, Spiritual Direction and Meditation, The Wisdom of the Desert

1961   *The Behavior of Titans, The New Man, New Seeds of Contemplation*

1962   *Clement of Alexandria, Original Child Bomb, A Thomas Merton Reader*

1963   Awarded medal for excellence by Columbia University
          Breakthrough to Peace, Emblems of a Season of Fury, Life and Holiness

1964   Honorary Doctorate of Letters, University of Kentucky
          Come to the Mountain, Seeds of Destruction

1965   August 20: formally enters the hermitage
        *Gandhi on Non-Violence, Seasons of Celebration, The Way of
        Chuang Tzu*

1966   *Conjectures of a Guilty Bystander, Hagia Sophia, Raids on
        the Unspeakable*

1967   *Mystics and Zen Masters*

1968   January 13: election of Abbot Flavian Burns
        May: visits California and Arizona
        September: visits Alaska, California, Asia
        December 10: dies in Bangkok, Thailand
        *Cables to the Ace, Faith and Violence, Zen and the Birds of
        Appetite*

1969   *Climate of Monastic Prayer* (later published as *Contem-
        plative Prayer*), *The Geography of Lograire, My Argument
        with the Gestapo, The True Solitude*

1970   *Opening the Bible*

1971   *Contemplation in a World of Action, Early Poems:
        1940–1941, Thomas Merton on Peace*

1972   *The Asian Journal of Thomas Merton, Cistercian Life*

1973   *Pasternak-Merton Letters*

1975   *He Is Risen*

1976   *Ishi Means Man*

1977   *The Collected Poems of Thomas Merton, A Hidden Wholeness*
        (with John Howard Griffin), *The Monastic Journey*

1978   *A Catch of Anti-Letters* (with Robert Lax)

1979   *Letters from Tom, Love and Living*

1980   *Thomas Merton on Saint Bernard*

1981   *Day of a Stranger, Introductions East and West, The Literary Essays of Thomas Merton*

1983   *Woods Shore, Desert*

1985   *The Hidden Ground of Love: Letters on Religious Experience and Social Concern* (Letters 1)

1986   *The Alaskan Journal of Thomas Merton*

1988   *A Vow of Conversation: Journals 1964–1965; Thomas Merton in Alaska: The Alaskan Conferences, Journals and Letters*

1989   *The Road to Joy: Letters to New and Old Friends* (Letters II), *Honorable Reader: Reflections on My Work*

1990   *The School of Charity: The Letters of Thomas Merton on Religious Renewal and Spiritual Direction* (Letters III)

1992   *The Springs of Contemplation*

1993   *The Courage for Truth: Letters to Writers* (Letters IV)

1994   *Witness to Freedom: Letters in Times of Crisis* (Letters V), *The Ways of the Christian Mystics*

1995   *Run to the Mountain: The Story of a Vocation* (Journals I: 1939–1941), *At Home in the World: The Letters of Thomas Merton and Rosemary Radford Ruether, Passion for Peace: The Social Essays*

1996   *Entering the Silence: Becoming a Monk and Writer* (Journals II: 1941–1952); *A Search for Solitude: Pursuing the Monk's True Life* (Journals III: 1952–1960); *Turning Toward the World: The Pivotal Years* (Journals IV: 1960–1963)

1997   *Dancing in the Water of Life: Seeking Peace in the Hermitage* (Journals V: 1963–1965); *Learning to Love: Exploring Solitude and Freedom* (Journals VI: 1966–1967); *Solitude and Love of the World; Thomas Merton and James Loughlin:*

Select Letters; *Straining Towards Being: The Letters of Thomas Merton and Czeslaw Milocz*

1998   *The Other Side of the Mountain: The End of the Journey* (Journals VII)

1999   *The Intimate Merton: His Life from His Journals*

2000   *Thomas Merton: Essential Writings*

2001   *Dialogues with Silence: Prayers and Drawings*; *When Prophecy Still Had a Voice: The Letters of Thomas Merton and Robert Lax*

2002   *Advent and Christmas with Thomas Merton*; *Survival or Prophecy? The Letters of Thomas Merton and Jean LeClerq*

2003   *Seeking Paradise: The Spirituality of the Shakers*; *When the Trees Say Nothing: Writings on Nature*

Acknowledgments

Excerpts from . . .

The Asian Journals of Thomas Merton, copyright © 1975 by The Trustees of the Merton Legacy Trust, reprinted by permission of New Directions Publishing Corp.

The Collected Poems of Thomas Merton, reprinted by permission of New Directions Publishing Corp.:
"The Communion"; "The Trappist Abbey: Matins"
copyright © 1944 by Our Lady of Gethsemani Monastery.
"And the Children of Birmingham"; "The Biography"
copyright © 1946 by New Directions Publishing Corporation.
"Abude-Harlem"; "Hagia Sophia: Section I"; "On the Anniversary of My Baptism"; "The Poet, To His Book"
copyright © 1948 by New Directions Publishing Corporation.
"To the Immaculate Virgin, On A Winter Night"
copyright © 1949 by Our Lady of Gethsemani Monastery.
"Elias—Variations on a Theme" (27 line excerpt);
"The Guns of Fort Knox"
copyright © 1957 by The Abbey of Gethsemani.
"Original Child Bomb"
copyright © 1962 by The Abbey of Gethsemani.
"Cables to The Ace: Sections 52, 82"; "Prologue"
copyright © 1968 by The Abbey of Gethsemani.
"The Strife between the Poet and Ambition"
copyright © 1968 by Thomas Merton.
"Cargo Songs"; "CHEESE"; "Ghost Dance: Prologue"; "Psalm 132: A Modern Monastic Revision"; "The Geography of Lograire: Author's Note"; "The Geography of Lograire, Prologue: The Endless Inscription" (Secions 1-3, 15-18)
copyright © 1968, 1969 by The Trustees of the Merton Legacy Trust.
"Hymn of Not Much Praise for New York City"
copyright © 1977 by The Trustees of the Merton Legacy Trust.
"Antipoem I"; "April 4th 1968"; "Paper Cranes"; "Picture of a Black Child with a White Doll"
copyright © 1977 by The Trustees of the Merton Legacy Trust.

Conjectures of a Guilty Bystander by Thomas Merton, copyright © 1966 by The Abbey of Gethsemani, reprinted by permission of Doubleday, a division of Random House, Inc.